History 4
Student Guide

Part 1

About K12 Inc.

K12 Inc. (NYSE: LRN) drives innovation and advances the quality of education by delivering state-of-the-art digital learning platforms and technology to students and school districts around the world. K12 is a company of educators offering its online and blended curriculum to charter schools, public school districts, private schools, and directly to families. More information can be found at K12.com.

978-1-60153-316-6

Printed by LSC Communications, Kendallville, IN, USA, May 2019.

Table of Contents

Unit 5: The Industrial Revolution

Unit 6: The Growth of Nations

Student Guide
Lesson 1. Optional: Maps and Globes: Directions and Hemispheres

Maps, globes, and satellite images give us a good picture of the Earth. Concepts such as scale and cardinal directions help us put maps to use. They also help us travel around the world and back in time as we study history.

Globes, maps, and satellite images are important tools that help us understand the Earth. Map keys help unlock the information on maps and imaginary lines help us navigate the globe.

Lesson Objectives

- Identify the seven continents and four oceans.
- Use cardinal and intermediate directions to interpret information on maps.
- Use map keys to interpret information on maps.
- Analyze political maps to gain information.
- Distinguish between absolute and relative location.
- Use lines of latitude and longitude to identify location.
- Use map scale to calculate distances between places,
- Identify different kinds of information provided by a globe, a map, and a satellite image.
- Locate specified places relative to the Equator, prime meridian or Earth's hemispheres.
- Demonstrate mastery of important geographic knowledge and skills.

PREPARE

Approximate lesson time is 60 minutes.

Keywords and Pronunciation

cardinal directions : The four main directions (north, south, east, and west).

compass rose : A symbol showing the directions on a map.

continent : One of the seven large areas of land on Earth.

Equator : An imaginary line around the middle of the Earth, halfway between the North and the South Poles.

hemisphere : One half of the Earth; the Earth can be divided into four hemispheres (Eastern, Western, Northern, and Southern).

intermediate directions : The directions in between the cardinal directions (northwest, northeast, southwest, and southeast).

map key : A guide to what the symobls on a map mean.

physical map : A map showing the Earth's natural features, such as rivers, lakes, and mountains.

prime meridian (priym muh-RIH-dee-uhn) : An imaginary line going around the Earth and running through the North and South Poles.

relative location : The location of one place in relation to another place.

satellite image : A picture of the Earth taken from space.

LEARN
Activity 1. Optional: Optional Lesson Instructions *(Online)*

Activity 2. Optional: Maps and Globes *(Online)*
Important historical events are frequently influenced by geography. It's time to take a look at the world. To get started, read the directions on the following screen.

Activity 3. Optional: Hemispheres and Directions *(Online)*

ASSESS
Optional. Wrap-Up: Maps and Globes: Directions and Hemispheres (*Online*)
You will complete an offline assessment covering the main objectives of this lesson. Your learning coach will score this assessment.

Lesson Assessment

Maps and Globes: Directions and Hemispheres

1. Which shows the true shape of the continents—a map or a globe?

    A. globe

    B. map

2. Label each Location on the map.

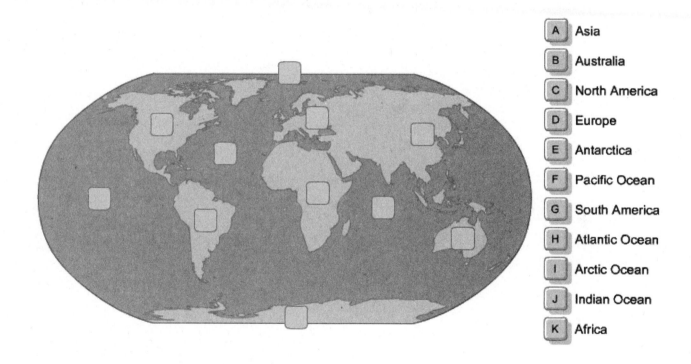

A	Asia
B	Australia
C	North America
D	Europe
E	Antarctica
F	Pacific Ocean
G	South America
H	Atlantic Ocean
I	Arctic Ocean
J	Indian Ocean
K	Africa

3. You are in the northern part of North America and sail east. What is the first continent you will reach?

    A. Asia

    B. Africa

    C. South America

    D. Europe

4. **Use the map of Tokyo on page 8 of *Understanding Geography* to answer this question.**
   If you were taking a train to visit Hamarikyu Garden, at which station would you get off?

   A. Tokyo Station

   B. Shimbash Station

   C. Harajuku Station

5. **Use the map of Tokyo on page 8 of *Understanding Geography* to answer this question.**
   When you are visiting Aoyama Cemetery you decide to go to the Nezu Art Musem. Which direction must you go?

   A. northwest

   B. north

   C. southwest

   D. south

6. In which two hemispheres is Australia located?

   A. Northern and Western Hemispheres

   B. Northern and Eastern Hemispheres

   C. Southern and Eastern Hemispheres

Student Guide
Lesson 2: Political Maps and Map Scales

On political maps, colors and symbols guide you as you search for countries, states, and cities. But how big are the countries? How far apart are they? Scales will give you those answers.

Lesson Objectives

- Explore concepts to be addressed during the year in History 4.
- Identify political maps as those showing the borders of countries or states.
- Distinguish between countries and continents.
- Analyze political maps to gain information.
- Use a map scale to calculate distances between places.
- Distinguish between large-scale and small-scale maps.

PREPARE

Approximate lesson time is 60 minutes.

Advance Preparation

- It's important that you read the Course Introduction for History 4 before your student begins the course. You can find the course introduction at the beginning of the Political Maps and Map Scales lesson.

Materials

For the Student

Understanding Geography: Map Skills and Our World (Level 4)

History Journal

LEARN
Activity 1: Welcome to History 4 *(Online)*

Activity 2: Continents, Countries, and Capitals *(Online)*

Instructions

- Read and discuss Activity 3, "Continents, Countries, and Capitals," on pages 16–19 of Understanding Geography.
- Answer Questions 1–18 in your History Journal.
- If you have time, you may want to answer the Skill Builder Questions on page 19. They are optional.

Activity 3: Distances *(Online)*

Activity 4. Optional: Political Maps and Map Scale *(Online)*

ASSESS

Lesson Assessment: Political Maps and Map Scales (*Online*)

You will complete an online assessment covering the main objectives of this lesson. Your assessment will be scored by the computer.

Student Guide
Lesson 2: Political Maps and Map Scales

On political maps, colors and symbols guide you as you search for countries, states, and cities. But how big are the countries? How far apart are they? Scales will give you those answers.

Lesson Objectives

- Explore concepts to be addressed during the year in History 4.
- Identify political maps as those showing the borders of countries or states.
- Distinguish between countries and continents.
- Analyze political maps to gain information.
- Use a map scale to calculate distances between places.
- Distinguish between large-scale and small-scale maps.

PREPARE

Approximate lesson time is 60 minutes.

Advance Preparation

- It's important that you read the Course Introduction for History 4 before your student begins the course. You can find the course introduction at the beginning of the Political Maps and Map Scales lesson.

Materials

For the Student

Understanding Geography: Map Skills and Our World (Level 4)

History Journal

LEARN
Activity 1: Welcome to History 4 *(Online)*

Activity 2: Continents, Countries, and Capitals *(Online)*
Instructions

- Read and discuss Activity 3, "Continents, Countries, and Capitals," on pages 16–19 of Understanding Geography.
- Answer Questions 1–18 in your History Journal.
- If you have time, you may want to answer the Skill Builder Questions on page 19. They are optional.

Activity 3: Distances (Online)

Activity 4. Optional: Political Maps and Map Scale (Online)

ASSESS

Lesson Assessment: Political Maps and Map Scales (*Online*)

You will complete an online assessment covering the main objectives of this lesson. Your assessment will be scored by the computer.

Student Guide
Lesson 3: Grids Show the Way

Can you think of a time when it would have been helpful to know exactly where you were? Have you ever been with someone who had an accident? Did they call for help and try to describe their location? Landmarks can help. So can street names and route numbers. Geographers and satellites for global positioning systems use lines of latitude and longitude to locate places.

Lesson Objectives
- Express or identify a location using longitude and latitude.
- Identify lines of longitude and how they help determine location.
- Distinguish between absolute and relative location.
- Recognize that lines of latitude are also called parallels, and lines of longitude are also called meridians.
- Identify lines of latitude and how they help determine location.

PREPARE

Approximate lesson time is 60 minutes.

Materials
> For the Student
>> Understanding Geography: Map Skills and Our World (Level 4)
>> History Journal

Keywords and Pronunciation
degree : A unit of measure used to tell how far north or south of the Equator and east or west of the prime meridian a place is located.

latitude (LA-tuh-tood) : Parallel lines that run east and west on a map or globe and measure distance north and south.

longitude (LAHN-juh-tood) : Lines that run from the North Pole to the South Pole on a map or globe and measure distance east and west.

prime meridian (priym muh-RIH-dee-uhn) : An imaginary line that runs between the North and South Poles and divides the Earth into the Eastern and Western Hemispheres.

relative location : The location of one place in relation to another place.

LEARN
Activity 1: Grids Show the Way *(Offline)*

Instructions

Do you know exactly where you are? Follow the directions in the Student Guide to find out.

- Read and discuss Activity 5, "The Coordinate System," on pages 24–29 of Understanding Geography.
- Answer Questions 1–33 in your History Journal.
- If you have time, you may want to answer Questions 34–37 and the Skill Builder Questions on page 29. They are optional.

Activity 2: Grids Show the Way (Offline)

Instructions

How good are you at giving the geographic address of a place? Find out now.

Latitude and longitude are tools that people use to give a place's geographic "address." What geographic addresses can you identify?

Look at the map on pages 70–71 of Understanding Geography. Choose five or more of the cities on the map. Figure out their addresses. Write them down. Then challenge someone else to name each mystery city based on its address.

Here's an example. Find the city of Salem, Oregon (OR). Its address is 45° N, 123° W. All you would say is that the mystery place is 45° N, 123° W. It would be up to the other person to find out that it was Salem.

Suppose someone told you that another mystery place is at 35° N, 107° W. How quickly would you find Santa Fe, New Mexico?

Now make a list of your own. Challenge someone else to find the places using their geographic addresses.

ASSESS

Lesson Assessment: Grids Show the Way (Online)

You will complete an online assessment covering the main objectives of this lesson. Your assessment will be scored by the computer.

Student Guide
Lesson 1: What's So Modern About the Modern World?

Science, the organized study of how nature works, was born around the year 1600. Thinkers began to experiment and observe very carefully. Knowledge took giant leaps forward as scientists studied everything from the human body to the way planets move. Today we call that great period of learning the Scientific Revolution. It was the start of our modern world.

Modern means "of recent or present times." For historians, the "modern world" means the world of the last 400 years or so. Our modern world has seen huge leaps in medicine, technology, government, and scientific understanding.

Lesson Objectives

- Describe the Scientific Revolution as a time of great progress in understanding nature.
- Explain that scientists used new methods of experimentation, obversation, and mathematics to understand nature.
- State that the Scientific Revolution began around 1600 and continued through the 1700s.
- Identify key figures in the Scientific Revolution (Harvey, Hooke, Leeuwenhoek, Descartes, Newton, Franklin) and their contributions.
- Explain that people gained confidence in their ability to understand the laws of nature.
- Define *modern* as meaning "of recent times."
- Explain that for historians "the modern world" means the world since the 1600s.
- Name some characteristics of the modern world, such as advances in medicine, health, communication, transportation, democracy, free speech, and space travel.
- Recognize the Scientific Revolution as the period beginning in 1600 when thinkers began to use experimentation, observation, and mathematics to understand the workings of nature.
- Interpret historical maps to gain information.

PREPARE

Approximate lesson time is 60 minutes.

Materials

For the Student

Understanding Geography: Map Skills and Our World (Level 4)

History Journal

Keywords and Pronunciation

Scientific Revolution : A time of great progress in science. The Scientific Revolution began in the 1600s.

LEARN
Activity 1: The Scientific Revolution *(Online)*
Get ready to learn about an amazing and wonderful revolution!

Activity 2: History Journal *(Offline)*
Instructions
It's time to add another chapter to the story of the past. Follow the directions to complete a new entry in your History Journal.

Turn to a new page in your History Journal. On this page, write a paragraph that tells what the lesson was about.

Begin with a topic sentence that introduces the paragraph. Include at least three sentences that give details about the lesson. End with a concluding sentence. You may use the Show You Know questions to help you get started.

When you have finished, check your work. Make sure you have written in complete sentences. Check to make sure you used correct capitalization and punctuation. Date your entry and label it with the lesson title.

Guided Learning: Compare your paragraph with the one in the Teacher Guide.

Activity 3: Then and Now *(Offline)*
Instructions
Here's another chance to compare the modern world with the past.

The modern world has been full of changes. Government has changed. Medicine has changed. Travel has changed. In this lesson, you remembered some of those changes.

Then you practiced comparing the way things were before 1600 with the way they are now. You thought about tall buildings, photography, and the ways people study the moon and stars.

Now it's time to create some more comparisons between the modern world and the past. Here are a few topics to get you started.

- Dentistry
- Sports
- Education
- Entertainment

Before 1600, people did not go to the dentist regularly. Now...

Before 1600, people played and watched some sports. But not the way they do today. Now...

Before 1600, most people did not go to school. This was especially true for women. Now...

Before 1600, there was no radio or TV. There were no movies or video games. Now...

Add some comparisons of your own. Choose one to illustrate, if you like. Share your observations with someone else. Invite that person to add more.

Activity 4: Focus on Geography *(Offline)*
Instructions
People in the fifteenth and sixteenth centuries were very curious about the world. Kings and queens wanted to claim new lands, and adventurers were eager to explore unknown lands and fill in the map of the world. Historical maps can tell us about events that happened long ago or show us what people in the past thought places looked like. To learn more about historical maps:

- Read pages 56–57 of Understanding Geography.
- Answer Questions 1–9 in your History Journal.
- When you have finished, compare your answers to the ones in the Teacher Guide.
- You will be assessed on this geography information after you finish the Historical Maps activity in the next lesson.

ASSESS

Lesson Assessment: What's So Modern About the Modern World? (*Online*)
You will complete an online assessment covering the main objectives of this lesson. Your assessment will be scored by the computer.

Student Guide
Lesson 2: William Harvey Gets to the Heart of Things

Meet William Harvey, an English doctor who showed how blood circulates in mammals. Harvey discovered that the heart works like a pump. It makes blood flow through arteries to the body and through veins back to the heart. His work became the basis for understanding the human heart and blood vessels.

Lesson Objectives

- Clearly explain in complete sentences that William Harvey was an English physician who discovered that blood circulates.
- Explain that William Harvey discovered the heart works like a pump to circulate blood.
- State that William Harvey used the scientific method.
- Interpret historical maps to gain information.

PREPARE

Approximate lesson time is 60 minutes.

Materials

>   For the Student
>
>   >   History Journal
>   >
>   >   Understanding Geography: Map Skills and Our World (Level 4)

Keywords and Pronunciation

arteries : vessels that carry blood away from the heart.

blood vessels : Tiny pipes through which blood flows in the human body. Two kinds of blood vessels are arteries and veins.

cadavers (kuh-DA-vurs)

historical map : Map that tells about events that happened in the past.

scientific method : A way to find answers by experimenting, observing, and drawing conclusions.

veins : vessels that carry blood toward the heart

LEARN
Activity 1: In Circulation (Online)

An imaginary lecture by William Harvey explains his remarkable thinking about blood, the heart, and the circulatory system.

Activity 2: History Journal *(Offline)*

Instructions

Pretend you are a reporter getting ready to write an article on William Harvey. A good reporter takes notes. You can "sit in" on Harvey's lecture and note the highlights.

Get ready to write an article about William Harvey's lecture. Go back and review the online book The Argument, in the activity titled In Circulation. In your journal, write down some of the key ideas. You will use them in the next activity.

Remember to choose the things that will help you inform the readers of your article the most. Be sure to note the date and the lecture title. Try to answer all of these questions:

- Who was William Harvey?
- What did he discover?
- What did Harvey say about the heart and what it does?
- What did he do to test and prove his ideas?

Which of these ideas did you write in your journal? Before you write your article, add any others that you want from this list.

- William Harvey was an English doctor.
- Harvey was the personal doctor for King Charles.
- Harvey explained that the heart works like a pump.
- Harvey described how arteries and veins work.
- Harvey had experimented with animals. He had seen blood pumping.

Activity 3: Reporting on a Remarkable Discovery *(Offline)*

Instructions

You just sat in on William Harvey's lecture. Now it's time to report on it.

Imagine that you're a reporter. For this assignment, you must travel back in time to see and hear William Harvey's lecture in 1627.

Use the notes in your History Journal to write an article about his discoveries for your local paper. Be sure to explain how the audience reacted to Harvey's words. Write your article clearly in complete sentences.

If you do the Beyond the Lesson activity, you may want to add a diagram to your article.

Activity 4: Focus on Geography *(Offline)*

Instructions

Maps can be useful tools to track the spread of disease. Historical maps show how the Black Death spread across Europe during the Middle Ages.

To find out more about historical maps:

- Finish reading Activity 12, "Historical Maps," pages 58–59, in *Understanding Geography*.
- Answer Questions 10–19 in your History Journal.
- When you have finished, compare your answers to the ones in the Teacher Guide.

ASSESS

Lesson Assessment: William Harvey Gets to the Heart of Things, Part 1

(*Online*)

You will complete an online assessment covering the main objectives of this lesson. Your assessment will be scored by the computer.

Lesson Assessment: William Harvey Gets to the Heart of Things, Part 2

(*Online*)

Have an adult review your essay and input the results in the assessment at the end of the lesson.

LEARN

Activity 5. Optional: William Harvey Gets to the Heart of Things *(Online)*

Instructions

Learn more about the history of the heart and circulation. Visit the Franklin Institute online.

Lesson Assessment

William Harvey Gets to the Heart of Things, Part 2

Get ready to write an article about William Harvey's lecture. Imagine that you're a reporter and you must travel back in time to see and hear William Harvey's lecture in 1627. Go back and review the online book *The Argument*, in the activity titled In Circulation. In your journal, write down some of the key ideas.

Remember to choose the things that will help you inform the readers of your article the most. Be sure to note the date and the lecture title. Try to answer all of these questions:

- Who was William Harvey?
- What did he discover?
- What did Harvey say about the heart and what it does?
- What did he do to test and prove his ideas?

Use the notes in your History Journal to write an article about his discoveries for your local paper. Be sure to explain how the audience reacted to Harvey's words. Write your article clearly in complete sentences.

Student Guide
Lesson 3: What's Under That Microscope?

Galileo's telescope helped him look more closely at the planets and stars. Another tool helped scientists look more closely at tiny living things. Learn more about two scientists, Robert Hooke and Anton van Leeuwenhoek. Then take a look at what they saw with this amazing new tool—the microscope.

Lesson Objectives

- Describe the microscope as an important invention that helped scientists understand small life forms.
- State that Robert Hooke used an early form of the microscope.
- Describe Anton van Leeuwenhoek as one of the first people to record observations of microscopic life.
- Identify major physical features on the Earth.
- Use a landform map to identify physical features.

PREPARE

Approximate lesson time is 60 minutes.

Materials

> For the Student
>> History Journal
>> Understanding Geography: Map Skills and Our World (Level 4)

Keywords and Pronunciation

adapt : To change or adjust your life to fit the world around you.

animalcules (a-nuh-MAL-kyools) : Anton van Leeuwenhoek´s term for tiny organisms. It means "little animals".

Anton van Leeuwenhoek (AHN-tohn vahn LAY-ven-hook)

cape : A part of the land that sticks into the sea.

coastal plain : A flat area between ocean and higher land.

hill : A raised area on Earth, not as high as a mountain.

landform : A physical feature on the Earth, such as a mountain, hill, or island.

lens : A piece of clear glass with curved surfaces that can make an image look larger.

mountain : The tallest type of landform, higher than a hill.

peninsula : A body of land that sticks out and is almost completely surrounded by water.

piedmont : An area of land at the foot of a mountain range.

plain : An area of mostly flat land.

plateau (pla-TOH) : An area of high, flat land.

LEARN

Activity 1: Leeuwenhoek Takes a Closer Look (Online)

Activity 2: History Journal (Offline)

Activity 3: Focus on Geography (Online)

ASSESS

Lesson Assessment: What's Under That Microscope? (Online)

You will complete an online assessment covering the main objectives of this lesson. Your assessment will be scored by the computer.

LEARN

Activity 4. Optional: What's Under the Microscope (Online)

Student Guide
Lesson 4: A Fly on the Ceiling: The Story of Cartesian Coordinates

Meet René Descartes, a Frenchman who changed our ideas about math and philosophy. He thought of a new system to help describe where objects are. People still use the Cartesian coordinate system today.

Lesson Objectives

- Identify René Descartes as a French mathematician and philosopher.
- Describe Cartesian coordinates as a way of locating any object on a graph.
- Explain that Descartes's system was a great advance in mathematics.
- Use a map to identify physical features.

PREPARE

Approximate lesson time is 60 minutes.

Materials

For the Student

Understanding Geography: Map Skills and Our World (Level 4)

History Journal

Keywords and Pronunciation

Anton van Leeuwenhoek (AHN-tohn vahn LAY-ven-hook)

archipelago (ahr-kuh-PEH-luh-goh) : A group of islands in a large body of water.

Cartesian (kahr-TEE-zhuhn)

island : Land that is completely surrounded by water.

isthmus (IS-muhs) : A narrow piece of land that connects to larger land areas.

René Descartes (ruh-NAY day-KAHRT)

LEARN
Activity 1: Descartes and Cartesian Coordinates *(Online)*

Activity 2: History Journal *(Offline)*

Activity 3: Using Cartesian Coordinates *(Online)*

Activity 4: Focus on Geography *(Online)*

ASSESS

Lesson Assessment: The Fly on the Ceiling: The Story of Cartesian Coordinates, Part 1 *(Online)*

You will complete an online assessment covering the main objectives of this lesson. Your assessment will be scored by the computer.

Lesson Assessment: The Fly on the Ceiling: The Story of Cartesian Coordinates, Part 2 *(Offline)*

Have an adult review your answers in the History Journal activity and input the results online.

LEARN

Activity 5. Optional: A Fly on the Ceiling: The Story of Cartesian Coordinates

(Online)

Lesson Assessment

The Fly on the Ceiling: The Story of Cartesian Coordinates, Part 2

1. Who was Rene Descartes? _____

2. What did Rene Descartes invent that was a great advance in mathematics? _____

3. What is Descartes's invention used for? _____

Student Guide
Lesson 5: Young Isaac Newton

Isaac Newton was a curious child. He liked to observe things closely, and he had many interests. He spent long hours studying nature. He built machines and thought about how the world worked. As a young man, he experimented with light and optics. And he puzzled over gravity.

Lesson Objectives

- Identify Isaac Newton as a great English scientist.
- Describe Newton as an observant and curious child.
- Tell about one of young Isaac Newton's experiments.
- Identify and distinguish different kinds of bodies of water.
- Identify and locate bodies of water on maps.
- Identify and define the source and mouth of rivers.

PREPARE

Approximate lesson time is 60 minutes.

Materials

For the Student

🖳 Newton Apple Mobile, Part 1

Understanding Geography: Map Skills and Our World (Level 4)

History Journal

Keywords and Pronunciation

Anton van Leeuwenhoek (AHN-tohn vahn LAY-ven-hook)

bay : A small body of water partly surrounded by land; usually smaller than a gulf.

fjord (fee-AWRD) : A narrow inlet from the sea between cliffs.

gulf : A part of a sea or ocean that extends into the land; usually larger than a bay.

lake : A body of water, usually freshwater, surrounded by land on all sides.

mouth : The end of a river, where it flows into a larger body of water.

ocean : One of four large bodies of salt water on Earth.

René Descartes (ruh-NAY day-KAHRT)

river : A large stream of freshwater that flows over land.

sea : A body of salt water that is smaller than an ocean.

source : The beginning of a river.

strait (strayt) : A narrow body of water connecting two larger bodies of water.

LEARN
Activity 1: Young Isaac Newton (Online)

Activity 2: History Journal (Offline)

Activity 3: Newton Apple Mobile (Online)

Activity 4: Focus on Geography (Online)

Activity 5. Optional: Young Isaac Newton (Online)

Newton Apple Mobile, Part 1

Each apple represents a time during Newton's life. Write a sentence or two on each apple to describe Newton during the time the apple represents. Cut the apples out and set them aside until the next lesson. You will finish this activity then.

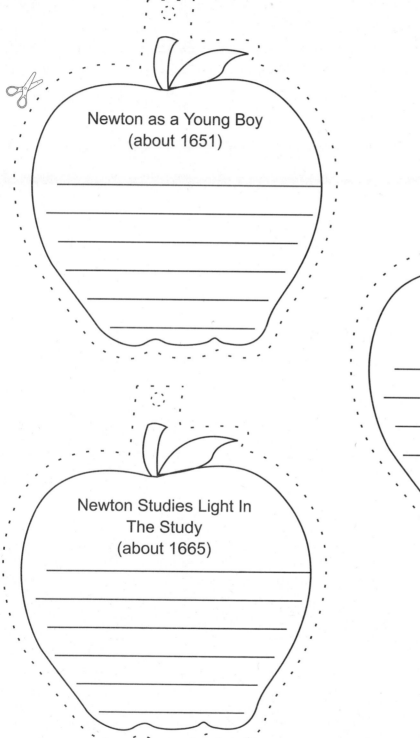

Newton as a Young Boy
(about 1651)

Newton Studies Light In
The Study
(about 1665)

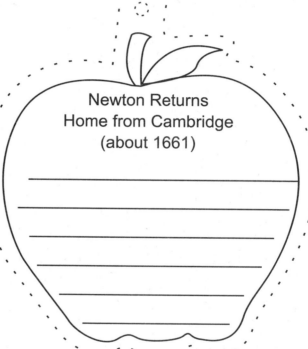

Newton Returns
Home from Cambridge
(about 1661)

Student Guide
Lesson 6: A New Kind of Knight

Isaac Newton discovered laws of gravity and motion. And he changed the way people looked at the world. Thanks to him, people began to see the universe as a place ordered by simple laws. They came to believe that human beings could understand the laws of nature. Newton was knighted for his discoveries.

Lesson Objectives

- Recognize that Isaac Newton discovered laws of gravity and motion.
- Explain that because of Newton's work, people began to think of the universe as a place that followed basic laws of nature.
- Explain that Newton's work gave people confidence that they could understand how the universe worked if they experimented, observed things closely, and thought carefully.
- Identify and distinguish different kinds of bodies of water.
- Define source and mouth of a river.
- Identify and locate bodies of water on maps.
- Demonstrate mastery of knowledge and skills from previous lessons.

PREPARE

Approximate lesson time is 60 minutes.

Materials

For the Student

- Newton Apple Mobile, Part 2
- scissors, round-end safety
- Understanding Geography: Map Skills and Our World (Level 4)
- History Journal

Keywords and Pronunciation

bay : A small body of water partly surrounded by land; usually smaller than a gulf.

fjord (fee-AWRD) : A narrow inlet from the sea between cliffs.

gravity : The force that pulls objects toward the Earth. It also keeps planets in orbit around the sun.

gulf : A part of a sea or ocean that extends into the land; usually larger than a bay.

lake : A large body of water, usually fresh, surrounded by land.

mouth : The end of a river, where it flows into a larger body of water.

ocean : One of four large bodies of salt water on Earth.

Principia (prin-SIH-pee-uh)

river : A large stream of freshwater that flows over land.

sea : A body of salt water that is smaller than an ocean.

source : The beginning of a river.

spectrum : A band of different colors formed when white light is separated by a prism. The spectrum has the same colors as a rainbow.

strait (strayt) : A narrow body of water connecting two larger bodies of water.

LEARN
Activity 1: Newton Is Knighted *(Online)*

Activity 2: History Journal *(Offline)*

Activity 3: Newton Apple Mobile *(Online)*

Activity 4: Focus on Geography *(Online)*

ASSESS
Lesson Assessment: A New Kind of Knight (*Online*)

You will complete an online assessment covering the main objectives of this lesson. Your assessment will be scored by the computer.

LEARN
Activity 5. Optional: A New Kind of Knight *(Online)*

Newton Apple Mobile, Part 2

Write a sentence or two on each apple to describe Newton during the time the apple shows. Cut the apples out. Gather the three apples from the last lesson. Attach all six apples to hangers or wooden dowels to make a mobile.

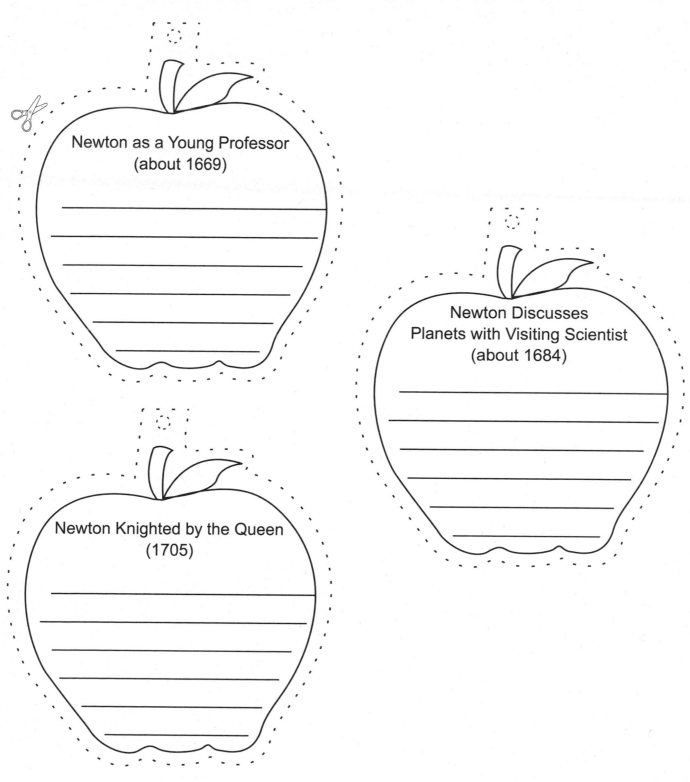

Newton as a Young Professor
(about 1669)

Newton Discusses
Planets with Visiting Scientist
(about 1684)

Newton Knighted by the Queen
(1705)

Student Guide
Lesson 7: Curious Ben Franklin

Benjamin Franklin was an American statesman. He was also a thinker and inventor. Franklin was widely admired in Europe. He was curious. He was intelligent. And he had many interests. He gave the world the lightning rod, bifocals, and the Franklin stove.

Lesson Objectives

- Describe Benjamin Franklin as a scientist and inventor with many interests.
- Explain that Benjamin Franklin conducted experiments on electricity and proved that lightning is really electricity.
- List some of Benjamin Franklin's inventions (lightning rod, bifocals, Franklin stove).

PREPARE

Approximate lesson time is 60 minutes.

Keywords and Pronunciation

Anton van Leeuwenhoek (AHN-tohn vahn LAY-ven-hook)
Principia (prin-SIH-pee-uh)

LEARN
Activity 1: Scientific Revolutionary *(Online)*

Activity 2: History Journal *(Online)*

Activity 3. Optional: Curious Ben Franklin *(Online)*

Student Guide
Lesson 8. Optional: Diderot's Revolutionary Encyclopedia

It was the Age of Reason. The Scientific Revolution was in full swing. Thinkers were learning more and more about their world. But how could they gather and record what they knew? Denis Diderot had an answer. He published an encyclopedia. It came out between 1751 and 1772. It had 28 volumes. It compiled current knowledge and thought. And it was revolutionary in its scope and ideas.

Lesson Objectives

- Identify Denis Diderot as a man in love with ideas and knowledge.
- Describe Diderot as the editor of the first modern encyclopedia.
- Explain that the encyclopedia helped spread ideas and knowledge about science.
- Explain that the encyclopedia encouraged people to ask questions and think for themselves.
- Demonstrate mastery of important knowledge and skills taught in this lesson.

PREPARE

Approximate lesson time is 60 minutes.

Keywords and Pronunciation

Denis Diderot (duh-nee DEE-duh-roh)

LEARN
Activity 1. Optional: Optional Lesson Instructions *(Online)*

This lesson is OPTIONAL. It is provided for students who seek enrichment or extra practice. You may skip this lesson.

If you choose to skip this lesson, then go to the Plan or Lesson Lists page and mark this lesson "Skipped" in order to proceed to the next lesson in the course.

Activity 2. Optional: Diderot Organizes Everything *(Online)*

Activity 3. Optional: History Journal *(Offline)*

Activity 4. Optional: Write an Encyclopedia Article on Diderot *(Online)*

Activity 5. Optional: Diderot's Revolutionary Encyclopedia *(Online)*

Student Guide
Lesson 9: Unit Review and Assessment

You've completed this unit, and now it's time to review what you've learned and take the unit assessment.

Lesson Objectives

- Demonstrate mastery of important knowledge and skills in this unit.
- Express or identify a location using longitude and latitude.
- Recognize the Scientific Revolution as the period beginning in 1600 when thinkers began to use experimentation, observation, and mathematics to understand the workings of nature.
- Explain that William Harvey discovered the heart works like a pump to circulate blood.
- Describe the microscope as an important invention that helped scientists understand small life forms.
- Describe Anton van Leeuwenhoek as one of the first people to record observations of microscopic life.
- Identify René Descartes as a French mathematician and philosopher.
- Describe Newton as an observant and curious child.
- Recognize that Isaac Newton discovered laws of gravity and motion.
- Explain that Newton's work gave people confidence that they could understand how the universe worked if they experimented, observed things closely, and thought carefully.
- Explain that Benjamin Franklin conducted experiments on electricity and proved that lightning is really electricity.
- List some of Benjamin Franklin's inventions (lightning rod, bifocals, Franklin stove).
- Use a landform map to identify physical features.
- Describe the Scientific Revolution as a time of great progress in understanding nature.
- State that the Scientific Revolution began around 1600 and continued through the 1700s.
- Explain that people gained confidence in their ability to understand the laws of nature.

PREPARE

Approximate lesson time is 60 minutes.

LEARN
Activity 1: Introducing the Modern World: The Scientific Revolution (Offline)
Instructions

We've covered a lot, and now it's time to take a look back. Here's what you should remember about the Scientific Revolution.

Our modern world speeds along. We race about in cars and planes. We send messages across continents in seconds. We get live pictures from distant lands on our TVs and computers. The world doesn't spin any faster than before. But it feels as if it did!

It all began with a Scientific Revolution. William Harvey wanted to know: How does the human body work? Others asked: What do the smallest parts of life look like? Descartes wanted to know: How can math help us describe the things? Newton wanted to know--well, Newton wanted to know just about everything! What is light? What is gravity? Why do planets move the way they do? How can math help us figure out the answers?

What was new and different about these people and their work? They wondered about nature in an organized way. They used what we call the scientific method. They did experiments and made careful observations. They wrote their observations down. They used math as it had never been used before. They even invented new kinds of math. They used new instruments such as the telescope and microscope. Suddenly human understanding of nature shot forward.

Let's review. We've been talking about a great Scientific Revolution. A revolution is a really big change. When did this Scientific Revolution begin? [1]

In the 1600s, some real geniuses were around. Let's start with William Harvey. He was English, and he was King James's doctor. What did William Harvey discover about blood? [2] What did he learn about the heart? [3]

Harvey wasn't the only one interested in living things. Another Englishman, Robert Hooke, invented a microscope. He saw plant cells for the first time. A Dutchman named Leeuwenhoek put together a better microscope. Do you remember what he saw? [4]

Careful observation helped Leeuwenhoek figure many things out. What did he do after he observed things under his microscope? [5]

Meanwhile, a great thinker was working in France. Do you remember his name? [6]

René Descartes especially loved math. He thought math could help people figure everything out. What did he figure out with his Cartesian coordinates? [7]

Meanwhile in England, a lonely little boy was reading Descartes's books. Do you remember his name? (Here's a hint: those science detectives, Sherman and Shirley, visited him.) [8]

Isaac Newton grew up to be one of the greatest scientists ever. What do you think of when you think of Newton? Light? Gravity? Motion? Math? Newton did great work in all those areas. He thought nature followed basic laws. People could figure these laws out. Newton made complicated things seem simple. People got very excited about his discoveries. The queen was so excited that she made him a knight.

Was there any limit to what human beings could learn? Ben Franklin didn't think so! In America, young Franklin was busy trying to figure things out. Remember his experiment with a kite? What did he prove? [9] Franklin's curiosity knew no limits. He worked with optics. He ground lenses to make excellent glasses. He invented a stove that gave more heat. Can you guess what that stove is called? [10]

During the Scientific Revolution, people were learning many new things in a short time. How could thinkers keep track of it all? Remember Diderot? What did he do? [11]

Diderot wanted to make sure that all the new knowledge was in one place. In 28 volumes, he collected it all. Well, not all--but a lot.

Whew! What an age. Hundreds of years earlier, people had thought mostly about heaven and life after death. It was an Age of Faith. Now people were thinking a lot about nature and life on this earth. People started to call their time an Age of Reason. Reason is careful thought.

Now, put your reason to the test! After you've given all of this some careful thought, review some more in the next two activities. Then go on to the assessment.

Activity 2: History Journal Review (Offline)

Instructions

It's time to prepare for the unit assessment by reviewing your History Journal.

Use your History Journal to review the unit called Introducing the Modern World: The Scientific Revolution. Take some time to go over the work you've done.

Guided Learning: An adult can also help you review by asking you questions based on the work in your journal.

Activity 3: Online Interactive Review (Online)

ASSESS

Unit Assessment: Introducing the Modern World: The Scientific Revolution

(*Online*)

You will complete an online assessment of the main objectives covered so far in this unit. Follow the instructions online. Your assessment will be scored by the computer.

Student Guide
Lesson 1: John Locke Spells Out the Laws of Good Government

Liberty. Democracy. The rights of man. Those words kindled flames in men's hearts in the late 1700s. They sparked two great revolutions. In America, colonists won their independence from England and founded a republic. Across the ocean, the French people started a revolution of their own. These two democratic experiments had very different results.

You've learned how the first real scientists began to understand the laws of nature. At about the same time, John Locke tried to figure out the laws of good government. Locke was an English political philosopher. He spoke up for the rights of the people. Later, his ideas would inspire the British colonists in North America.

Lesson Objectives

- Name the American and French Revolutions as two great democratic revolutions.
- Describe the growing importance of ideas about inalienable rights, the right of revolution, and leaders deriving power from the people.
- Describe a constitution as the basic law of government, which sets up the form of the government.
- Recognize that the U.S. Constitution employs three branches of government and a system of checks and balances.
- Describe three stages of the French Revolution (monarchy, republic, empire).
- Describe the Terror as a time of violence when many "enemies of the revolution" were killed.
- Explain that the French Revolution led to major European wars.
- Identify key figures, documents, and events in the American and French Revolutions (John Locke, Thomas Jefferson, James Madison, George Washington, Lafayette, Louis XVI, Robespierre, Napoleon, the Declaration of Independence, the U.S. Constitution, storming the Bastille, the Napoleonic Code, Waterloo).
- Describe John Locke as an English political philosopher.
- Explain that Locke taught that everyone has rights, and that rulers must follow important laws of good government.
- Explain that Locke believed the power to rule a nation came from the nation's people.
- Explain that Locke believed that if rulers governed badly, the people had a right of revolution.
- Use relief maps to identify and compare elevations of selected locations.
- Explain that elevation is height above sea level.

PREPARE

Approximate lesson time is 60 minutes.

Materials

For the Student

Understanding Geography: Map Skills and Our World (Level 4)

History Journal

Keywords and Pronunciation

elevation : The height of the land above sea level, also called *altitude*.

Glorious Revolution : A bloodless transfer of power to William and Mary in England. It established that Parliament was supreme.

philosopher : A person who seeks wisdom.

relief map : A map that shows the higher and lower parts of an area.

sea level : The level of the ocean; the elevation at sea level is 0 feet.

Thames (temz)

LEARN
Activity 1: The Right of Revolution *(Online)*

Activity 2: A Letter About Locke *(Offline)*
Instructions

Think back to the story The Philosopher and the Princess. In this story, John Locke explains his ideas on government to Princess Mary. Mary is on her way to London. There she will join her husband, William. The English Parliament is going to crown William and Mary king and queen of England.

Pretend you are a passenger on the boat. You overhear the conversation between John Locke and Princess Mary. You are excited by what you hear. So you decide to write a letter to a friend. Your friend also has ideas about government. You think he would be interested in Locke's ideas.

In your History Journal, write a friendly letter to this person. Start by describing John Locke to your friend. Who was he? What did he do? Then explain Locke's ideas on government. To refresh your memory, read the story again. For a date on your letter, use February 12, 1689.

Label this History Journal entry with today's date and the lesson title.

Continue to see the format of a friendly letter.

A friendly letter has five parts:
- Heading: the date
- Greeting: the name of the person you're writing to
- Body: the place where your message is written
- Closing: the place where you say good-bye
- Signature: your name

Here's an example of the format of a friendly letter:

Heading (date)

Greeting,

Body (Indent the first line. this is where you write your message.)

Closing

Signature

Activity 3: Focus on Geography *(Online)*
Instructions

Do you live at sea level or high up in the mountains? Relief maps can help you figure out the elevation of your region. How high up you live really influences your weather. Today we'll take a look at how elevation affects climate.

- Begin Activity 8, "Elevation and Relief Maps," by reading and discussing pages 40–41 of *Understanding Geography*.
- Answer Questions 1–7 in your History Journal.
- When you have finished, compare your answers to the ones in the Teacher Guide.
- You will be assessed on this geography information when you finish Activity 8 in the next lesson.

ASSESS

Lesson Assessment: John Locke Spells Out the Laws of Good Government
(*Online*)

Have an adult review your essay and input the results in the assessment at the end of the lesson.

Lesson Assessment

John Locke Spells Out the Laws of Good Government

Think back to the story The Philosopher and the Princess. In this story, John Locke explains his ideas on government to Princess Mary. Mary is on her way to London. There she will join her husband, William. The English Parliament is going to crown William and Mary king and queen of England.

Pretend you are a passenger on the boat. You overhear the conversation between John Locke and Princess Mary. You are excited by what you hear. So you decide to write a letter to a friend. Your friend also has ideas about government. You think he would be interested in Locke's ideas.

Start by describing John Locke to your friend. Who was he? What did he do? Then explain Locke's ideas on government. To refresh your memory, read the story again. For a date on your letter, use February 12, 1689.

A friendly letter has five parts:

- Heading: the date
- Greeting: the name of the person you're writing to
- Body: the place where your message is written
- Closing: the place where you say good-bye
- Signature: your name

Here's an example of the format of a friendly letter:

Heading (date)

Greeting,

Body (Indent the first line. This is where you write your message.)

Closing,
Signature

Student Guide
Lesson 2: Thomas Jefferson and the Declaration of Independence

British colonists in North America read John Locke's work. They read his ideas on government. They read about the right of revolution. And many of them agreed with him. In 1776, Thomas Jefferson wrote America's Declaration of Independence. It used many of Locke's words and ideas. Americans chose to make their new nation a republic. They based it on the idea that "all men are created equal."

Lesson Objectives

- Explain that Americans defended their right of revolution using some of John Locke's ideas.
- Identify Thomas Jefferson as the author of the Declaration of Independence.
- Recognize that the words "we hold these truths to be self-evident, that all men are created equal" come from the Declaration of Independence.
- State that the United States became a republic.
- Use relief maps to identify and compare elevations of selected locations.
- Explain that elevation is height above sea level.

PREPARE

Approximate lesson time is 60 minutes.

Materials

> For the Student
>> Understanding Geography: Map Skills and Our World (Level 4)
>> History Journal

Keywords and Pronunciation

delegate (DEH li guht) : A representative to a convention or conference.

elevation : The height of the land above sea level, also called *altitude*.

independence : Freedom from control by others.

relief map : A map that shows the higher and lower parts of an area.

republic : A government in which citizens elect representatives to govern according to laws.

sea level : The level of the ocean; the elevation at sea level is 0 feet.

self-evident : Obvious; clear and not needing proof.

tyrant : A ruler who has total power over people.

unalienable (uhn-AYL-yuh-nuh-buhl) : "Unalienable rights" are rights that cannot be taken away.

LEARN
Activity 1: Independence Declared! *(Online)*
John Locke had ideas about it. Ben Franklin talked about it. Thomas Jefferson wrote it.

Activity 2: History Journal (Offline)
Instructions

You read an imaginary talk between Jefferson and Franklin. What can you recall about it?

In the story, Thomas Jefferson and Benjamin Franklin talked about many important things. Copy the following sentences into your History Journal and fill in the blanks. This will help you remember some of the things Jefferson and Franklin talked about. Be sure to write the date and lesson title in your journal.

[1] Americans thought they had a right to be free. One reason they thought this was because of the words of an English political philosopher. His name was _____.

[2] Thomas Jefferson wrote an important document. It was called the _____.

[3] Thomas Jefferson thought anyone could see the truth of some of the things he wrote. He said these truths were _____.

[4] Jefferson made a number of important points. One was that "all men are created _____."

[5] The United States became a _____. This is a country with elected representatives who run the government.

Activity 3: Focus on Geography (Offline)
Instructions

Thomas Jefferson was a statesman, a thinker, and a writer. And he was much more than that. He was a Renaissance man like Leonardo da Vinci. While he worked on the Declaration of Independence, Jefferson also kept careful records of the weather. When he became president and doubled the size of the country by buying land from the French, he quickly sent explorers to gather information about the new land. Today you will explore the elevation of the United States.

- Read pages 42–43 of Activity 8, "Elevation and Relief Maps"
- Answer Questions 8–15 in your History Journal
- If you have time, you may want to answer the Skill Builder Questions on page 43. They are optional.
- When you have finished, compare your answers with the ones in the Teacher Guide.

ASSESS

Lesson Assessment: Thomas Jefferson and the Declaration of Independence, Part 1 (Online)

You will complete an online assessment covering the main objectives of this lesson. Your assessment will be scored by the computer.

Lesson Assessment: Thomas Jefferson and the Declaration of Independence, Part 2 (Online)

You will complete an offline assessment covering the main objectives of this lesson. Your learning coach will score this assessment.

LEARN
Activity 4. Optional: Thomas Jefferson and the Declaration of Independence
(Online)

Did Thomas Jefferson write a rough draft of the Declaration of Independence? See for yourself.

Lesson Assessment

Thomas Jefferson and the Declaration of Independence, Part 2

1. Americans thought they had a right to be free. One reason they thought this was because of the words of an English political philosopher. His name was _____.

2. Thomas Jefferson wrote an important document. It was called the _____.

3. Thomas Jefferson thought anyone could see the truth of some of the things he wrote. He said these truths were _____.

4. Jefferson made a number of important points. One was that "all men are created _____."

5. The United States became a _____. This is a country with elected representatives who run the government.

Student Guide
Lesson 3: James Madison and the U.S. Constitution

The young United States had a weak central government. The new nation faced uprisings in its early years. Americans thought hard about how to make their republic work. James Madison thought harder and better than most. He came to Philadelphia in 1787 with a plan.

Lesson Objectives

- Describe James Madison as the Father of the Constitution.
- Define *federal government* as a central government over all the states.
- Explain that James Madison studied history and knew that democracies usually didn't last long.
- Identify the Constitutional Convention as the meeting in which the United States made a new plan of government.
- Locate and identify major mountain ranges around the world.
- Identify selected mountain peaks.

PREPARE

Approximate lesson time is 60 minutes.

Materials

For the Student

glue, children's white non-toxic

paper, 8 1/2" x 11"

pencils, colored, 16 colors or more

scissors, round-end safety

Understanding Geography: Map Skills and Our World (Level 4)

History Journal

Keywords and Pronunciation

constitution (kahn-stuh-TOO-shuhn) : A document listing the powers and duties of a government.

delegate (DEH li guht) : A representative to a convention or conference.

mountain range : A large group of mountains.

physical map : A map showing the Earth's natural features, such as rivers, lakes, and mountains.

LEARN
Activity 1: A New Government *(Online)*

See how the U.S. government got its start.

Activity 2: History Journal *(Offline)*

Instructions

It's time to add another chapter to the story of our past. Create a new entry in your History Journal.

Turn to a new page in your History Journal. On this page, write a paragraph that tells what the lesson was about. Begin with a topic sentence that introduces the paragraph. Include at least three sentences that give details about the lesson. End with a concluding sentence. You may use the Show You Know questions to help you get started.

When you have finished, check your work. Make sure you have written in complete sentences. Check to make sure you used correct capitalization and punctuation. Now click Answers to see a sample paragraph. Compare this paragraph with yours. Did you include the most important parts of the lesson? Date your entry and label it with the lesson title.

Activity 3: A Home Page for James Madison *(Online)*

Design James Madison's home page.

Activity 4: Focus on Geography *(Offline)*

Instructions

There are mountains on every continent. To learn about some of the major mountain ranges around the world:

- Read page 44 of Activity 9, "Mountains," in *Understanding Geography*
- Answer Questions 1–11 in your History Journal.
- When you have finished, compare your answers with the ones in the Teacher Guide.
- You will be assessed on this geography information after you finish Activity 9 in the next lesson.

ASSESS

Lesson Assessment: James Madison and the U.S. Constitution *(Offline)*

You will complete an online assessment covering the main objectives of this lesson. Your assessment will be scored by the computer.

LEARN

Activity 5. Optional: James Madison and the U.S. Constitution *(Online)*

Instructions

Visit these websites together to learn more about the U.S. Constitution.

Student Guide
Lesson 4: George Washington and the American Presidency

George Washington became president in 1789. This was the first great test of the U.S. Constitution. The American people loved Washington. But could a president become a king? What did it mean to be the president of the United States?

Lesson Objectives

- Explain that many Americans feared their strong president might become a king.
- Describe George Washington as a leader Americans trusted.
- Name two ways that George Washington helped put people's fears to rest (clothing, manners, title, stepping down after two terms).
- Locate and identify major mountain ranges around the world.
- Identify selected mountain peaks.
- Describe how people adapt to living in mountainous regions.

PREPARE

Approximate lesson time is 60 minutes.

Materials

    For the Student
        Understanding Geography: Map Skills and Our World (Level 4)
        History Journal

Keywords and Pronunciation

mountain range : A large group of mountains.

physical map : A map showing the Earth's natural features, such as rivers, lakes, and mountains.

LEARN
Activity 1: The First President of the United States *(Online)*

Activity 2: History Journal *(Online)*
Instructions

It's time to add another chapter to the story of our past. Create a new entry in your History Journal.

Activity 3: The Many Jobs of the President (Online)

Does the president have one job or many different jobs? See for yourself.

Activity 4: Focus on Geography (Offline)

Instructions

To explore the mountains in France and learn how people adapt to living in the mountains:

- Read pages 45–47 of Activity 9, "Mountains," in *Understanding Geography*.
- Answer Questions 12–16 in your History Journal.
- If you have time, you may want to answer the Skill Builder Questions on page 47. They are optional.
- When you have finished, compare your answers with the ones in the Teacher Guide.

ASSESS

Lesson Assessment: George Washington and the American Presidency
(*Online*)

You will complete an online assessment covering the main objectives of this lesson. Your assessment will be scored by the computer.

Student Guide
Lesson 5: The U.S. Constitution: Three Branches of Government

The U.S. Constitution set up rules for the nation's government. The government has three branches. Each branch has its own functions and powers. The legislative branch makes laws. The executive branch carries out the laws. The judicial branch explains what the laws mean and settles disagreements about them.

Lesson Objectives

- Explain that the U.S. Constitution established rules for a government over all the states.
- State that the Constitution divides power among three branches of government.
- Name and describe at least one power of each of the three branches of government.

PREPARE

Approximate lesson time is 60 minutes.

Materials

For the Student

The U.S. Constitution and You by Syl Sobel

📖 The Three Branches of Government activity sheet

📖 The Three Branches of Government answer sheet

Keywords and Pronunciation

branch of government : One part of the government.

executive branch : The branch of government that carries out the laws. The president is the head of the executive branch.

judicial branch : The branch of government that explains the laws and settles disagreements about them. The judicial branch includes the Supreme Court and other federal courts.

legislative branch : The branch of government that makes the laws. It includes Congress, which is made up of the Senate and the House of Representatives.

LEARN
Activity 1: The Three Branches of Government *(Online)*

Instructions

How is the U.S. government set up? Read to find out about all the key parts.

Activity 2: History Journal *(Online)*

Instructions

It's time to add another chapter to the story of our past. Create a new entry in your History Journal.

Activity 3: The Three Branches of Government *(Offline)*

Do you remember the parts and people of the three branches of government?

Activity 4. Optional: The U.S. Constitution: Three Branches of Government

(Online)

There's so much to know about the three branches of government. Here's a website that will help.

ASSESS

Lesson Assessment: The U.S. Constitution: Three Branches of Government

(Online)

You will complete an online assessment covering the main objectives of this lesson. Your assessment will be scored by the computer.

Name _____

Date _____

The Three Branches of Government

Use the word bank to label the parts or people in each of the three branches of government. There are more words in the bank than you will need, so choose carefully.

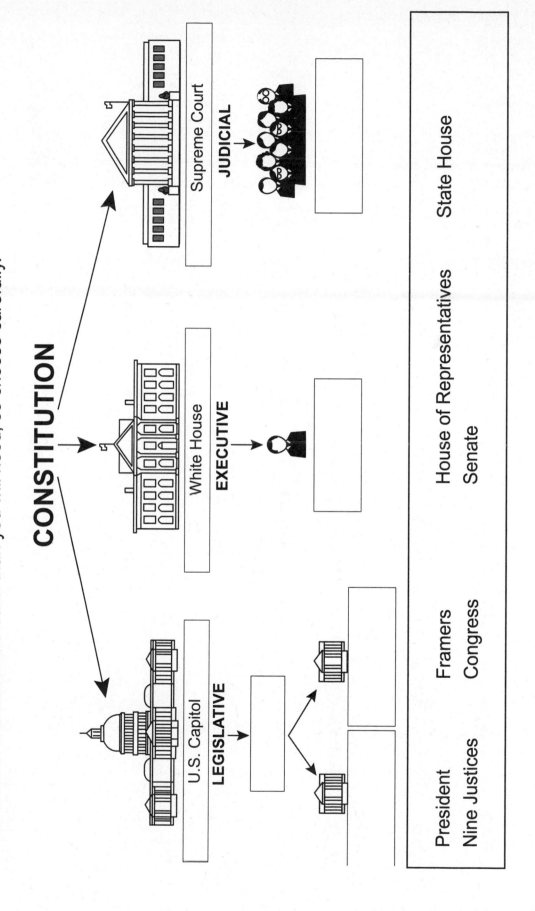

CONSTITUTION

U.S. Capitol
LEGISLATIVE

White House
EXECUTIVE

Supreme Court
JUDICIAL

| President | Framers | House of Representatives | State House |
| Nine Justices | Congress | Senate | |

The Three Branches of Government

Use the word bank to label the parts or people in each of the three branches of government. There are more words in the bank than you will need, so choose carefully.

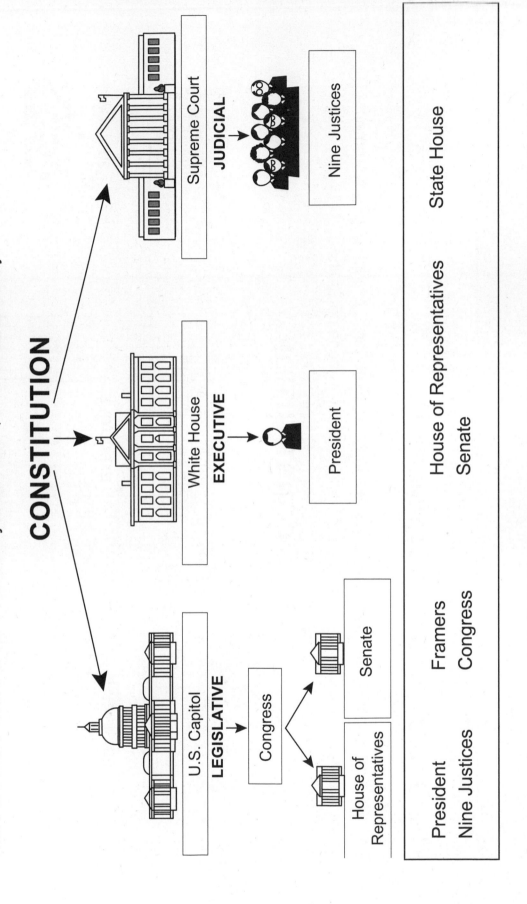

President	Framers	House of Representatives	State House
Nine Justices	Congress	Senate	

Student Guide
Lesson 6: The U.S. Constitution: Checks and Balances

Each branch of the U.S. government has some power over the others. Called checks and balances, these powers serve an important purpose. They make sure that no part of the government has too much power over the others. The Constitution established these checks. The Constitution can only be changed by a special process called amendment.

Lesson Objectives

- Define *checks and balances* as powers each branch of government has over the others.
- Name one check that the president has over Congress, that Congress has over the president, and that the Supreme Court has over Congress.
- Define *veto* as a presidential power to reject a law passed by Congress.
- Explain that the Constitution can only be changed by amendment.

PREPARE

Approximate lesson time is 60 minutes.

Materials

> For the Student
>> The U.S. Constitution and You by Syl Sobel

Keywords and Pronunciation

amendment : A change; for example, a change to the Constitution.

checks and balances : Powers each branch of government has to control or limit the power of another branch of government.

impeach : To charge a government official with doing wrong.

veto : The presidential power to reject a law passed by Congress.

LEARN
Activity 1: Checks and Balances *(Online)*

How did the Constitution set up the U.S. government so that it would keep running smoothly?

Activity 2: History Journal *(Online)*

It's time to add another chapter to the story of our past. Create a new entry in your History Journal.

Instructions

It's time to add another chapter to the story of our past. Create a new entry in your History Journal.

Activity 3: Checks or Balances? *(Online)*

Activity 4. Optional: The U.S. Constitution: Checks and Balances *(Online)*

The Constitution describes some important rights that belong to every citizen. Learn more about these rights.

ASSESS

Lesson Assessment: The U.S. Constitution: Checks and Balances (*Online*)

You will complete an online assessment covering the main objectives of this lesson. Your assessment will be scored by the computer.

Student Guide
Lesson 7: Rumblings of Revolution in France

Democratic ideals soon spread to France. France had a king, Louis XVI. And he had great powers. But this began to change. The king called together the Estates General. The people demanded a constitution for France. The French Revolution had begun.

Lesson Objectives

- Identify Louis XVI as the French king at the time of the French Revolution.
- Explain that French kings believed they ruled by divine right.
- Using complete sentences, explain that the French people were eager for a constitution that would give them a say in government.
- Identify the members of the Third Estate as people who were neither nobles nor clergy.

PREPARE

Approximate lesson time is 60 minutes.

Materials

> For the Student
>> crayons, 64 colors or more
>>
>> paper, 8 1/2" x 11"
>>
>> pencils, colored, 16 colors or more

Keywords and Pronunciation

debt : Something owed.

Estates General : The French congress. It consisted of three different groups (estates).

Louis (LOO-ee)

Marie Antoinette (muh-REE an-twuh-NET)

Marquis de Lafayette (mahr-KEE duh lah-fee-ET)

oath (OHTH) : A promise.

philosophes (fee-luh-ZAWFS)

LEARN
Activity 1: Setting the Stage for Another Revolution *(Online)*

Activity 2: A Session in Court *(Online)*
An oath on a tennis court? What's that all about?

Activity 3: History Journal *(Online)*

Instructions

It's time to add another chapter to the story of our past. Create a new entry in your History Journal.

Activity 4. Optional: Rumbling the Revolutions in France *(Online)*

Instructions

Want to see where Louis XVI and Marie Antoinette lived? Take a virtual tour of their palace at Versailles.

ASSESS

Lesson Assessment: Rumblings of Revolution in France (*Online*)

Have an adult review your essay and input the results in the assessment at the end of the lesson.

Lesson Assessment

Rumblings of Revolution in France

Write a paragraph that tells what the Rumblings of Revolution in France lesson was about. Begin with a topic sentence that introduces the paragraph. Include at least three sentences that give details about the lesson. End with a concluding sentence.

Be sure to include the king's name, including the Roman numeral. Explain what he thought about the rights of kings. Remember to mention the Third Estate and explain what it was.

Student Guide
Lesson 8: Storming the Bastille!

The French king, Louis XVI, was worried about the new National Assembly. The people were worried about Louis XVI. They thought royal arms were stored at the Bastille. On July 14, 1789, they stormed the Bastille, and the French Revolution began. The French celebrate Bastille Day as a national holiday.

Lesson Objectives

- Identify the Bastille as a prison or fortress.
- Describe the Bastille as a hated symbol of royal power to many people in France.
- Explain that on July 14, 1789, a large crowd stormed the Bastille.
- Use complete sentences to explain that Bastille Day is a national holiday in France and is regarded as the start of the French Revolution.

PREPARE

Approximate lesson time is 60 minutes.

Materials

For the Student

paper, 8 1/2" x 11"

pencils, colored, 16 colors or more

Keywords and Pronunciation

Bastille (bah-STEEL) : A royal fortress in Paris.

Pierre (pee-EHR)

LEARN
Activity 1: The Revolution Takes to the Streets (Online)
See how a prison played a part in the French Revolution.

Activity 2: History Journal (Offline)
Instructions
It's time to add another chapter to the story of our past. Create a new entry in your History Journal.

Turn to a new page in your History Journal. On this page, write a paragraph that tells what the lesson was about. Your work will be used to assess how well you understood the lesson.

Begin with a topic sentence that introduces the paragraph. Include at least three sentences that give details about the lesson. End with a concluding sentence. You may use the Show You Know questions to help you get started.

When you have finished, check your work. Make sure you have written in complete sentences. Check to make sure you used correct capitalization and punctuation. Date your entry and label it with the lesson title.

Guided Learning: Compare your paragraph with the one in the Lesson Guide.

Activity 3: Storming the Bastille: A Day to Remember *(Online)*

Get out your pencils! It's time to draw a political cartoon. How can you show the main ideas about the storming of the Bastille?

Activity 4. Optional: Storming the Bastille *(Online)*

Visit the French embassy and learn more about Bastille Day.

ASSESS

Lesson Assessment: Storming the Bastille! (*Online*)

Have an adult review your essay and input the results in the assessment at the end of the lesson.

Name _____   Date _____

Lesson Assessment

Storming the Bastille!

Write a paragraph that tells what the Storming the Bastille! lesson was about.

Begin with a topic sentence that introduces the paragraph. Include at least three sentences that give details about the lesson. End with a concluding sentence. You may use the Show You Know questions to help you get started.

When you have finished, check your work. Make sure you have written in complete sentences. Check to make sure you used correct capitalization and punctuation.

Student Guide
Lesson 9: Farewell, Louis: From Monarchy to Republic

The French Revolution brought a new constitution. It limited the powers of the king, Louis XVI. He and his wife, Marie Antoinette, tried to flee France. They were arrested. Later, they were beheaded. With its king gone, France became a republic.

Lesson Objectives

- Explain that Louis XVI was arrested and later beheaded.
- Describe Louis XVI as opposed to changes that limited the king's power.
- Explain that France changed from a monarchy to a republic.

PREPARE

Approximate lesson time is 60 minutes.

Materials

> For the Student
>> History Journal

Keywords and Pronunciation

constitution (kahn-stuh-TOO-shuhn) : A document listing the powers and duties of a government.

guillotine (GIH-luh-teen)

Marie Antoinette (muh-REE an-twuh-NET)

Vive la république (veev lah ray-poob-leek)

Vive le roi (veev luh rwa)

LEARN
Activity 1: King Louis XVI Loses His Head *(Online)*

The storming of the Bastille let Louis XVI know the people of France wanted change. Then what happened?

Activity 2: Why Didn't Louis Last? *(Offline)*

Instructions

Did you wonder why Louis didn't last? Take some time to review the reasons for his unfortunate end.

Louis XVI was captured as he was leaving France. He was executed in 1793. Some of these statements correctly describe why he was captured. Others are incorrect. Copy the true statements into your History Journal. Title the page "The Execution of Louis XVI."

1. Louis XVI didn't really accept the new French constitution.
2. Louis XVI wanted people to recognize him on the way from France to Austria.
3. Marie Antoinette insisted on bringing so many things that they were noticed.
4. Louis XVI and Marie Antoinette took their time leaving and traveled slowly.

---

5. Louis XVI opposed the changes that limited his power as king of France.

6. Marie Antoinette wanted to eat very simple meals as quickly as possible.

7. Louis XVI's picture was on some French money, so it was easy to recognize him.

8. Louis XVI and Marie Antoinette understood the needs and wishes of the people.

9. Louis XVI tried to end the French Revolution by getting help from Austria.

10. Marie Antoinette tried to stop Louis from leaving.

Guided Learning: Check your answers against the Lesson Guide.

Activity 3. Optional: Farewell, Louis: From Monarchy to Republican (Online)

Take a multimedia tour of the French Revolution.

ASSESS

Lesson Assessment: Farewell, Louis: From Monarchy to Republic (Online)

You will complete an online assessment covering the main objectives of this lesson. Your assessment will be scored by the computer.

Student Guide
Lesson 10: The Terror!

The Terror was a time when leaders of the French Revolution thought they had to kill all their enemies. Robespierre was a famous leader of this time. Many people died on the guillotine.

Lesson Objectives

- Describe Robespierre as a revolutionary leader in France.
- Explain that Robespierre and the Committee of Public Safety used terror against supporters of the king and "enemies of the Revolution."
- Use complete sentences to describe the Terror as a period of terrible revolutionary violence in which many people who opposed the Revolution were killed.

PREPARE

Approximate lesson time is 60 minutes.

Keywords and Pronunciation

Liberté, égalité, fraternité (lee-behr-TAY, ay-ga-lee-TAY, fra-tehr-nee-TAY)

Maximilien Robespierre (mahk-see-meel-yan ROHBZ-pyehr)

LEARN
Activity 1: Fear Grips France *(Online)*

Activity 2: History Journal *(Offline)*
Instructions

It's time to add another chapter to the story of the past. Follow the directions to complete a new entry in your History Journal.

Turn to a new page in your History Journal. On this page, write a paragraph that tells what the lesson was about. Your work will be used to assess how well you understood the lesson.

Begin with a topic sentence that introduces the paragraph. Include at least three sentences that give details about the lesson. End with a concluding sentence. You may use the Show You Know questions to help you get started.

When you have finished, check your work. Make sure you have written in complete sentences. Check to make sure you used correct capitalization and punctuation. Date your entry and label it with the lesson title.

Guided Learning: Compare your paragraph with the one in the Teacher Guide.

Activity 3: Robespierre in Time *(Online)*

ASSESS
Lesson Assessment: The Terror! (*Online*)

Have an adult review your essay and input the results in the assessment at the end of the lesson.

LEARN
Activity 4. Optional: The Terror! (*Online*)

Lesson Assessment

The Terror!

Write a paragraph that tells what The Terror! lesson was about.

Begin with a topic sentence that introduces the paragraph. Include at least three sentences that give details about the lesson. End with a concluding sentence. You may use the Show You Know questions to help you get started.

When you have finished, check your work. Make sure you have written in complete sentences. Check to make sure you used correct capitalization and punctuation.

Student Guide
Lesson 11: The Rise of Napoleon

Napoleon Bonaparte started out as a young army officer. But he had great ambition. And he had a great military mind. He quickly rose to power. First he became a general. Then he became the leader of France. We still remember him as one of the greatest generals who ever lived.

Lesson Objectives

- Describe Napoleon as one of the greatest generals in history.
- Explain that Napoleon led French republican armies to victory in many parts of the world, and name two of these victories.
- Explain that military triumphs made Napoleon very popular in France.
- State that Napoleon became First Consul of France.

PREPARE

Approximate lesson time is 60 minutes.

Materials

For the Student

- Map of Napoleonic Europe
- Napoleon's Triumphs Activity Sheet

Keywords and Pronunciation

Attaque! Toujours l'attaque (uh-tahk! too-zhour lah-tahk!)
Corsica (KOR-sih-kuh)
Napoleon Bonaparte (nuh-POHL-yuhn BOH-nuh-pahrt)
Toulon (too-LAWN)

LEARN
Activity 1: France's Dashing Young General *(Online)*

See how a young army officer quickly rises to become a general and then the leader of France.

Activity 2: History Journal *(Offline)*
Instructions

It's time to add another chapter to the story of our past. Create a new entry in your History Journal.

Turn to a new page in your History Journal. On this page, write a paragraph that tells what the lesson was about.

Begin with a topic sentence that introduces the paragraph. Include at least three sentences that give details about the lesson. End with a concluding sentence. You may use the Show You Know questions to help you get started.

When you have finished, check your work. Make sure you have written in complete sentences. Check to make sure you used correct capitalization and punctuation. Date your entry and label it with the lesson title.

Guided Learning: Compare your paragraph with the one in the Teacher Guide.

Activity 3: Napoleon's Triumphs *(Online)*
Instructions

Napoleon led French armies to victory in many parts of the world. Complete the activity sheet to show where he went.

Guided Learning: When you finish, print the answer key and check your work.

ASSESS
Lesson Assessment: The Rise of Napoleon (*Online*)
You will complete an online assessment covering the main objectives of this lesson. Your assessment will be scored by the computer.

LEARN
Activity 4. Optional: The Rise of Napoleon *(Online)*

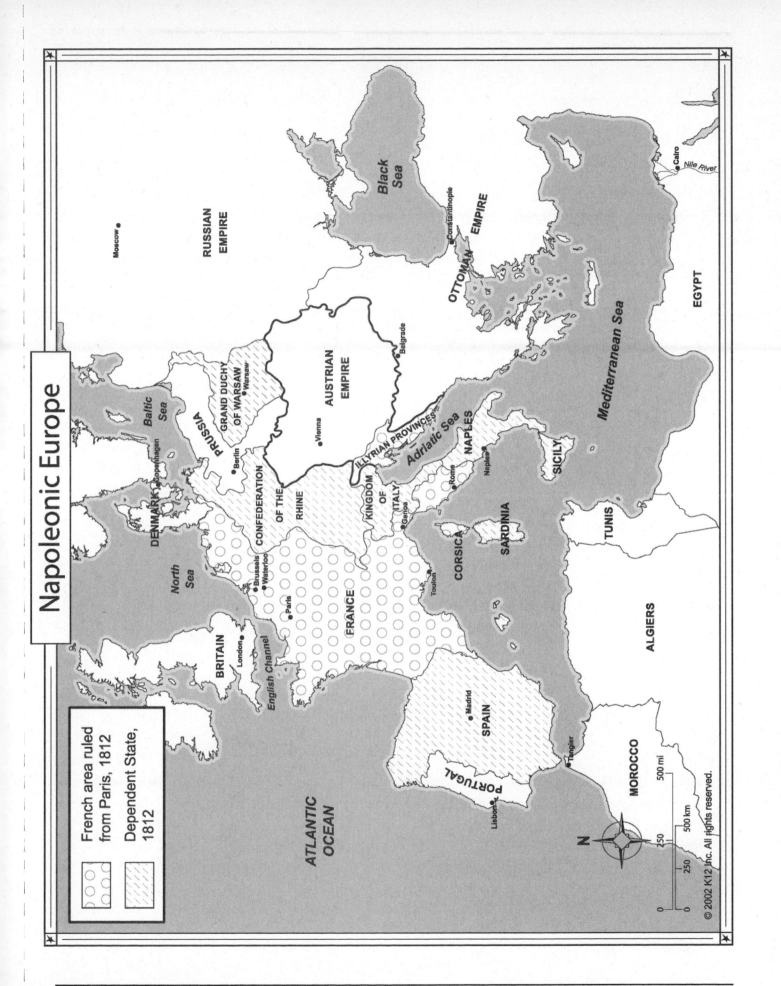

Napoleonic Europe

French area ruled from Paris, 1812

Dependent State, 1812

RUSSIAN EMPIRE

Moscow

Black Sea

OTTOMAN EMPIRE

Constantinople

Cairo

Nile River

EGYPT

Mediterranean Sea

PRUSSIA

GRAND DUCHY OF WARSAW

Warsaw

Berlin

AUSTRIAN EMPIRE

Vienna

Belgrade

Baltic Sea

Copenhagen

DENMARK

CONFEDERATION OF THE RHINE

ILLYRIAN PROVINCES

Adriatic Sea

KINGDOM OF ITALY

NAPLES

Naples

Rome

Genoa

North Sea

Brussels

Waterloo

Paris

FRANCE

BRITAIN

London

English Channel

Toulon

CORSICA

SARDINIA

SICILY

TUNIS

ALGIERS

ATLANTIC OCEAN

SPAIN

Madrid

PORTUGAL

Lisbon

Tangier

MOROCCO

N

500 mi

500 km

250

250

0

0

© 2002 K12 Inc. All rights reserved.

Name _____   Date _____

Napoleon's Triumphs

1. On the map, find the island where Napoleon Bonaparte was born. Label it with the island's name. Draw a star next to the island.

2. Find the dot that stands for the city of Toulon. Write the name of the city on the line next to it. What happened after a young artillery officer named Napoleon arrived in Toulon?

   _____

   _____

   _____

3. Find the dot that stands for the city of Paris. Write the name of the city on the line next to it. Why did the Directory order Napoleon to come to Paris?

   _____

   _____

4. Find Italy on the map and label it. Whom did Bonaparte defeat in Italy?

   _____

   What did he tell his soldiers during this bold campaign?

   _____

5. After Napoleon returned from Italy, he was sent off to do battle with another country. Circle that country.

6. Instead of attacking the country itself, Napoleon decided to attack one of its colonies. This was located in Africa. Where did Napoleon attack?

   _____

   Label this place on the map.

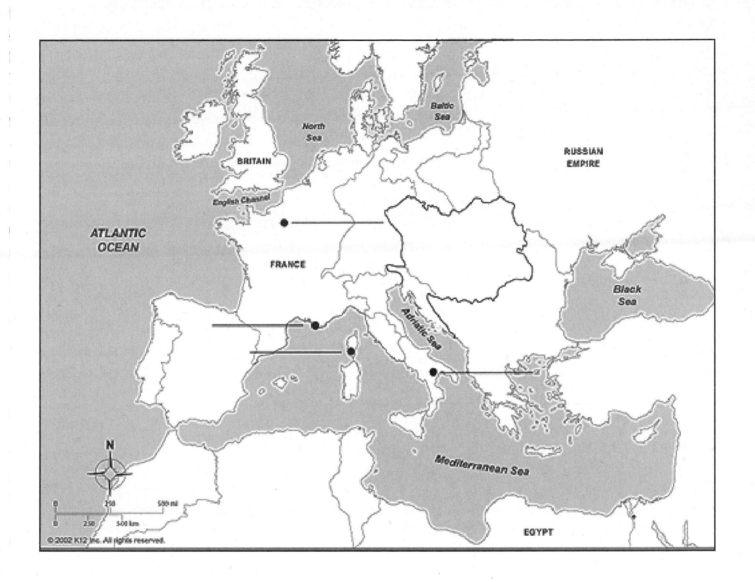

Student Guide
Lesson 12. Optional: Washington's Farewell: Stay Out of Europe's Wars

Americans were proud of their Revolution. They cheered when revolution spread to France. Should they help the French in their wars against the rest of Europe? Washington urged Americans to stay out of Europe's wars.

Lesson Objectives

- Explain that some Americans wanted the United States to help the French in their war against the rest of Europe.
- Describe the Farewell Address as the speech George Washington wrote when he left office.
- Describe the Farewell Address as a speech that said Americans should protect their liberty by staying out of European wars.

PREPARE

Approximate lesson time is 60 minutes.

Keywords and Pronunciation

levee (LEH-vee) : A formal reception for state visitors.

LEARN
Activity 1. Optional: Optional Lesson Instructions *(Online)*

This lesson is OPTIONAL. It is provided for students who seek enrichment or extra practice. You may skip this lesson.

If you choose to skip this lesson, then go to the Plan or Lesson Lists page and mark this lesson "Skipped" in order to proceed to the next lesson in the course.

Activity 2. Optional: Washington Says Farewell *(Online)*

Activity 3. Optional: History Journal *(Offline)*

Instructions

It's time to add another chapter to the story of the past. Follow the directions to complete a new entry in your History Journal.

Turn to a new page in your History Journal. On this page, write a paragraph that tells what the lesson was about. Your work will be used to assess how well you understood the lesson.

Begin with a topic sentence that introduces the paragraph. Include at least three sentences that give details about the lesson. End with a concluding sentence. You may use the Show You Know questions to help you get started.

When you have finished, check your work. Make sure you have written in complete sentences. Check to make sure you used correct capitalization and punctuation. Date your entry and label it with the lesson title.

Guided Learning: Compare your paragraph with the one in the Teacher Guide.

Activity 4. Optional: A Letter to the Editor (Offline)
Instructions

What did you think about Washington's advice to the country? Write a letter to the editor telling what you thought of his farewell speech.

Newspapers have a special section for opinions. It's called the editorial section. There you'll find articles written by newspaper writers. These articles tell you what the writers think about events. You'll also find letters to the editor. The people who read the newspaper write these letters. The letters tell you what the readers think.

Imagine you're living in Philadelphia. It's September 1796. You've just read Washington's Farewell Address. It was printed in a Philadelphia newspaper. Write a letter to the editor of this newspaper. Respond to what you've read.

In your letter, be sure to tell your readers:

- what different opinions Americans had about helping France in its war
- what the Farewell Address was
- what George Washington said about getting involved in Europe's war

You can praise the advice Washington gave in his speech. Or you can criticize it. Make sure you date your letter. The greeting should be "Dear Editor."

Activity 5. Optional: Washington's Farewell: Stay Out of Europe's Wars (Offline)
Instructions

Learn about a custom George Washington set when he was president. He created a cabinet.

George Washington set many precedents during his presidency. A *precedent* is an example for other people to follow. Washington was the first president. So he made up many of the customs of the presidency. He invented traditions as he went along. Many of the things he did as president are still done today.

Washington created the first presidential *cabinet.* What is a cabinet? You probably know one meaning of this word--a case or cupboard. But what does the word mean as it's used here?

Do some research. Find out what a cabinet is. How does it relate to the presidency? Use sources such as online or print encyclopedias and nonfiction library books. Take notes as you read.

After you've finished your research, write a paragraph. It should explain what a presidential cabinet is and what it does.

Student Guide
Lesson 13: Napoleon: Lawgiver and Emperor

As First Consul, Napoleon changed the face of France. His most important achievement was setting up an orderly set of laws. These laws were called the Napoleonic Code. But Napoleon also took more and more power for himself. In 1804, he crowned himself emperor. Now France was no longer a republic. It was an empire.

Lesson Objectives

- Explain that, after years of revolution and violence, the French wanted a strong leader.
- Describe Napoleon as the republican hero who became an all-powerful emperor.
- Describe the Napoleonic Code as Napoleon's greatest accomplishment.

PREPARE

Approximate lesson time is 60 minutes.

Materials

> For the Student
>> 🖥 Bonaparte and Caesar activity sheet
>> What's the Deal? Jefferson, Napoleon, and the Louisiana Purchase by Rhoda Blumberg

Keywords and Pronunciation

code : A system of law.

Vive l'Empereur (veev lahng-pehr-ehr)

LEARN
Activity 1: The Emperor and Lawgiver *(Online)*

Activity 2: Napoleon Bonaparte and Julius Caesar, Part 1 *(Offline)*
Instructions

Compare and contrast the empires and careers of Napoleon Bonaparte and Julius Caesar.

To *compare and contrast* is to note how two things are alike and different. Compare and contrast Napoleon and Caesar. How were these two men alike? How were they different? How were their empires alike, and how were they different?

If you're not familiar with Julius Caesar, you'll need to do a little research on this man from ancient Rome. Use an encyclopedia to learn about who he was and what he did. You may also want to revisit this lesson and the Rise of Napoleon lesson to review Napoleon's life and career.

You'll begin this activity today and finish it during the next lesson. Do your research today. Use any resources that you can find. Focus on what each of the two men did and what kind of empire he built. Take notes as you read. You'll begin the writing part of the activity during the lesson on Waterloo.

ASSESS

Lesson Assessment: Napoleon: Lawgiver and Emperor (*Online*)

You will complete an offline assessment covering the main objectives of this lesson. Your learning coach will score this assessment.

LEARN

Activity 3. Optional: Lawgiver and Emperor (*Offline*)

Instructions

What part did Napoleon play in the Louisiana Purchase? Find out in a well-written book by Rhoda Blumberg. Check your library or bookstore for *What's the Deal? Jefferson, Napoleon, and the Louisiana Purchase*, by Rhoda Blumberg. You'll learn about the event that transformed the United States "from a weak and vulnerable nation into a great power."

Name

Date

Note-taking Graphic Organizer

	Julius Caesar	Napoleon Bonaparte
Early Life		
Turning Point		
Military Experience		
Empires		

Lesson Assessment

Napoleon: Lawgiver and Emperor

1. After years of revolution and violence, what kind of leader did the French people

   want?_____

2. For a while, Napoleon was admired as a republican hero. What title did he end up giving

   himself?_____

3. What was Napoleon's greatest accomplishment?_____

Student Guide
Lesson 14: Waterloo!

As emperor of France, Napoleon began expanding his empire. Europe's kings and queens grew appalled at his conquests. Again and again they tried to defeat him in battle. At last he met Britain's Duke of Wellington at Waterloo. There Napoleon was defeated in one of the most famous battles of all time.

Lesson Objectives

- Explain that Napoleon had many conquests and built a vast empire.
- Identify Waterloo as the famous battle in which Napoleon was defeated.
- Identify the Duke of Wellington as the British hero who defeated Napoleon.
- Understand that the expression "meet your Waterloo" means to be defeated by something.

PREPARE

Approximate lesson time is 60 minutes.

Materials

For the Student

🖳 Map of Napoleonic Europe

Keywords and Pronunciation

plateau (pla-TOH) : A flat stretch of high land.

Vive l'Empereur (veev lahng-pehr-ehr)

LEARN

Activity 1: Master of Europe (Online)

Napoleon's empire grew and grew. When would it end?

Activity 2: Napoleon Bonaparte and Julius Caesar (Offline)

Instructions

Complete the activity you started in the last lesson.

In the last lesson, you did some research. You researched the careers and empires of Napoleon Bonaparte and Julius Caesar. Now it's time to turn your research into a short, two-paragraph written report.

The first paragraph should compare and contrast the careers of Bonaparte and Caesar. Remember, to *compare and contrast* is to note how two things are alike and different. Look at the notes you took during your research. What did each man do during his career? What were some things the two men did that were similar? What were some things that were different?

The second paragraph should compare and contrast the empires Bonaparte and Caesar built. How did they build their empires? How large were they? Did they conquer other countries to enlarge their empires? What happened to their empires when they fell from power?

Remember to begin each paragraph with a topic sentence. This sentence should introduce the main idea of the paragraph. Here's an example of a topic sentence for the first paragraph:

Although Napoleon Bonaparte and Julius Caesar lived during different times, they were alike in many ways. The rest of the paragraph will give specific details about how the two men were alike (and how they were different). End each paragraph with a concluding sentence.

ASSESS
Lesson Assessment: Waterloo! (*Offline*)
You will complete an online assessment covering the main objectives of this lesson. Your assessment will be scored by the computer.

LEARN
Activity 3. Optional: Waterloo! (*Online*)

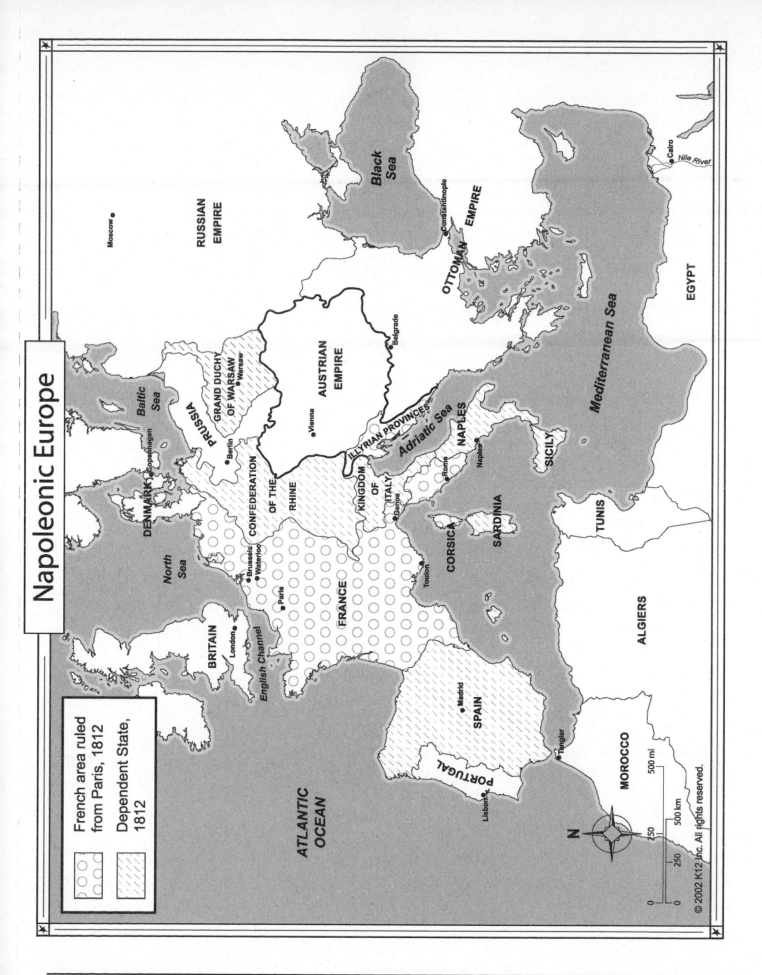

Napoleonic Europe

French area ruled from Paris, 1812

Dependent State, 1812

RUSSIAN EMPIRE

Moscow

Black Sea

AUSTRIAN EMPIRE

Vienna

Belgrade

OTTOMAN EMPIRE

Constantinople

Cairo

Nile River

EGYPT

Mediterranean Sea

GRAND DUCHY OF WARSAW

Warsaw

PRUSSIA

Berlin

Baltic Sea

DENMARK

Copenhagen

CONFEDERATION OF THE RHINE

ILLYRIAN PROVINCES

Adriatic Sea

KINGDOM OF ITALY

Genoa

Rome

NAPLES

Naples

SICILY

SARDINIA

CORSICA

Toulon

North Sea

BRITAIN

London

English Channel

Brussels

Waterloo

Paris

FRANCE

TUNIS

ALGIERS

Madrid

SPAIN

PORTUGAL

Lisbon

Tangier

MOROCCO

ATLANTIC OCEAN

N

500 mi

500 km

250

250

0

0

Student Guide
Lesson 15: Unit Review and Assessment

You've completed this unit, and now it's time to review what you've learned and take the unit assessment.

Lesson Objectives

- Demonstrate mastery of important knowledge and skills in this unit.
- Describe John Locke as an English political philosopher.
- Explain that Locke taught that everyone has rights, and that rulers must follow important laws of good government.
- Explain that Locke believed that if rulers governed badly, the people had a right of revolution.
- Identify Thomas Jefferson as the author of the Declaration of Independence.
- State that the United States became a republic.
- Describe James Madison as the Father of the Constitution.
- Identify the Constitutional Convention as the meeting in which the United States made a new plan of government.
- Explain that many Americans feared their strong president might become a king.
- State that the Constitution divides power among three branches of government.
- Name and describe at least one power of each of the three branches of government.
- Define *checks and balances* as powers each branch of government has over the others.
- Explain that the Constitution can only be changed by amendment.
- Identify Louis XVI as the French king at the time of the French Revolution.
- Describe Robespierre as a revolutionary leader in France.
- Explain that Robespierre and the Committee of Public Safety used terror against supporters of the king and "enemies of the Revolution."
- Describe Napoleon as one of the greatest generals in history.
- Describe Napoleon as the republican hero who became an all-powerful emperor.
- Describe the Napoleonic Code as Napoleon's greatest accomplishment.
- Identify the Duke of Wellington as the British hero who defeated Napoleon.
- Explain that on July 14, 1789, a large crowd stormed the Bastille.
- Name the American and French Revolutions as two great democratic revolutions.
- Describe a constitution as the basic law of government, which sets up the form of the government.
- Describe three stages of the French Revolution (monarchy, republic, empire).
- Describe the Terror as a time of violence when many "enemies of the revolution" were killed.
- Explain that the French Revolution led to major European wars.

PREPARE

Approximate lesson time is 60 minutes.

LEARN
Activity 1: Two Democratic Revolutions *(Offline)*

Instructions

We've covered a lot, and now it's time to take a look back. Here's what you should remember about these two great democratic revolutions.

Liberty. Democracy. The rights of man. Those words kindled flames in men's hearts in the late 1700s. They sparked two great revolutions--the American Revolution and the French Revolution. Those words are still lighting fires today.

John Locke may have started it all. Back in 1688, the English tossed out one king and invited another to rule instead. John Locke wrote a book saying the English had done a very good thing. All people have rights, he said. Kings don't get their power to rule from God. They get it from the people. If monarchs ignore the rights of the people, then the people should rise up and throw them out! That powerful idea became known as the right of revolution.

There came a time when the English king started ignoring the rights of colonists in America. The colonists remembered old John Locke. They thought, "Don't we have rights? Why should we be ruled by a king who ignores our rights? If we rule ourselves, we will have our liberty."

In 1776, American colonists declared independence from England. They started their own republic. Who wrote their Declaration of Independence? [1]

The Declaration of Independence said all people had rights. Can you name three of the rights it named? [2] With that document, Americans started their own country. And they declared a war. It became known as the American Revolution.

Americans won their Revolution. Then they faced the hard work of setting up a good government for a free people. Some governments might be too powerful. Others might be too weak. By 1787, American leaders were saying, "We'd better get this right. We want both liberty and order. We need a better government." So they came together to design a new government for their country. What was the name of this meeting? [3]

A constitution is the basic law of a nation. It sets up the form of government. An American thinker studied the constitutions of past republics. He came up with a plan for the new constitution. What was his name? (Here's a hint: We call him the Father of the Constitution.) [4]

The U.S. Constitution is still working today. It divides power into three branches. What are they? [5]

The U.S. Constitution also makes sure that each branch of the government has some power over the others. What is that system called? [6]

Across the Atlantic Ocean, the French started thinking about rights and liberty, too. Some of the French, like Lafayette, had fought in the American Revolution. When they got back to France, they had less patience with a king who ignored the rights of the people.

The French people were tired of a government in which the king, nobles, and church controlled everything. France was divided into three groups called estates. Do you remember which estate was the largest? [7]

The Third Estate included everyone who was not a noble or a church leader. Members of the Third Estate wanted a say in government. They wanted a constitution. So they gathered on a tennis court to insist on it.

What big event in 1789 showed Louis XVI that the French people were very serious? (Here's a hint: a big fortress became a big symbol.) [8]

The French Revolution exploded. It burned its way through France and across Europe. At first the French people just wanted a constitution, a share of power, and a better life. But Louis XVI tried to stop them. The French people decided he had to go. So what happened to Louis XVI? [9]

France went from being a monarchy to being a republic. By 1793, the French had as their slogan "liberté, egalité, fraternité." This means "liberty, equality, brotherhood." But not many people were feeling brotherly. Revolutionaries worried that they had lots of enemies. Leaders like Robespierre said that enemies of the Revolution should die. For more than a year, heads rolled in France. What was that terrible time called? [10]

One constitution followed the next in France. And the leaders didn't worry much about checks and balances. They just worried about staying in power.

Revolutionaries also worried about enemies of the French Revolution outside France. Kings and queens who were related to Louis were angry he had been killed. They wanted to stop the Revolution. What if these awful ideas about liberty spread to their countries? So Prussia, Austria, Spain, Russia, and Britain marched. Could France survive their combined forces?

A little corporal in the French army laughed in the face of those nations. What was his name? [11]

Napoleon Bonaparte led French revolutionary armies in Europe to victory after victory. The French were very proud of their amazing general. In fact, they were so proud that eventually they said, "Let's make him our leader." He became France's First Consul.

Napoleon rewrote constitution after constitution. He gave himself more and more power. He also rewrote France's laws. He gave the nation a single, useful code of laws. Do you remember what that was called? [12]

Eventually, Napoleon said, "I am too magnificent to be a mere consul. Make me emperor." Napoleon thought he was so magnificent that he should even crown himself. "After all," he thought, "who is more powerful than me?" So he crowned himself emperor.

The rest of the story is a sad one. French armies fought on. They won many victories, but they laid waste to much of Europe. French armies said they were spreading liberty and republicanism. But now France was led by a dictator who put his relatives on every throne.

After 15 years of war, European nations were exhausted. But they fought on. In the end, Napoleon was defeated. You might say he met his Waterloo. What was Waterloo? [13]

In 1815 Napoleon was taken prisoner. A king was put back on the throne of France. The French Revolution was over.

European kings didn't want to hear any more about liberty, democracy, and the rights of man. That American experiment across the Atlantic was doomed to fail, they said. Americans followed George Washington's advice. They decided to stay out of Europe's sad state of affairs. Two democratic revolutions had produced two different results. But the winds of change were just beginning to blow.

Activity 2: History Journal Review *(Offline)*

Instructions

It's time to prepare for the unit assessment by reviewing your History Journal.

Use your History Journal to review the unit called Two Democratic Revolutions. Take some time to go over the work you've done. An adult can also help you review by asking you questions based on the work in your journal.

Activity 3: Online Interactive Review *(Online)*

ASSESS

Unit Assessment: Two Democratic Revolutions (*Offline*)

Complete an offline Unit Assessment. Your learning coach will score this part of the Assessment.

Name _____   Date _____

Two Democratic Revolutions

Read each question and its answer choices. Fill in the bubble in front of the word or words that best answer each question.

1. What kind of government did the United States have after it declared independence?

   ⓐ   monarchy

   ⓑ   republic

   ⓒ   empire

   ⓓ   dictatorship

2. What happened at the Constitutional Convention in 1787?

   ⓐ   The Third Estate in France formed a new government.

   ⓑ   The United States declared independence from Great Britain.

   ⓒ   A large crowd stormed the Bastille and demanded a constitution.

   ⓓ   The United States made a new plan of government.

3. What is a constitution?

   ⓐ   the basic budget of a nation, establishing the limits of spending and debt

   ⓑ   a document that shows the borders of each state in the nation

   ⓒ   the statements that declare a colony's independence from its mother country

   ⓓ   the basic law of government, establishing the form of a country's government

4. How can the U.S. Constitution be changed?

   ⓐ   by three-fourths of the states voting for a new amendment

   ⓑ   by presidential decree of a new amendment

   ⓒ   by a majority vote of the United States Congress

   ⓓ   by unanimous decision of the United States Supreme Court

5. What event occurred on July 14, 1789, and is regarded as the start of the French Revolution?

   ⓐ   Napoleon's army was defeated at Waterloo.

   ⓑ   Louis XVI was beheaded.

   ⓒ   A large crowd stormed the Bastille.

   ⓓ   Robespierre was arrested.

6. What was the Terror?

   ⓐ   a time in Europe when monarchs began following laws of good government

   ⓑ   a time of violence in France when enemies of the revolution were killed

   ⓒ   the battle in which Napoleon was defeated by the British

   ⓓ   the warning by George Washington to stay out of Europe's wars

7. Choose the three stages that best describe the progress of the French Revolution:

   ⓐ   monarchy, republic, empire

   ⓑ   terror, monarchy, republic

   ⓒ   republic, monarchy, empire

   ⓓ   monarchy, Directory, Terror

8. What was the Napoleonic Code?

    ⓐ   a single set of new laws written for everyone in France

    ⓑ   rules for fighting wars that Napoleon followed in Europe

    ⓒ   France's first constitution after Louis XVI was beheaded

    ⓓ   a code of good behavior begun by Napoleon

9. What did John Locke believe and teach?

    ⓐ   Only nobles and royalty have rights.

    ⓑ   Monarchs have the power to get rid of Parliament.

    ⓒ   The power to rule a nation comes from God.

    ⓓ   If rulers govern badly, people have a right to overthrow them.

10. How did the French Revolution affect the rest of Europe?

    ⓐ   Many nations admired Napoleon and eagerly made him
          emperor.

    ⓑ   A period of wars followed as other rulers tried to stop the
          spread of revolutionary ideas.

    ⓒ   Some nations provided a new home for Louis XVI.

    ⓓ   It had almost no effect because the French people and armies
          kept to themselves.

11. Name two great democratic revolutions that occurred in the second
    half of the 1700s.

    _____

    _____

12. When the constitution was written, some Americans were worried about the office of the presidency. They thought that _____.

  ⓐ   the new president might not have enough power and be ineffective

  ⓑ   a president was likely to be dishonest

  ⓒ   the new president might have too much power and become king

  ⓓ   the president might not spend enough time on the nation's business

13. Which two groups make up the U.S. Congress, the legislative branch of the U.S. government?

  ⓐ   President and Cabinet

  ⓑ   Supreme Court and Senate

  ⓒ   House of Representatives and President

  ⓓ   Senate and House of Representatives

Match the name of each person on the left with a description of the person on the right. Write the letter of the description on the line in front of the name. (There is one extra description on the right that does not match any of the people on the left.)

14. _____ John Locke

    _____ Thomas Jefferson

    _____ James Madison

    _____ Louis XVI

    _____ Robespierre

    _____ Napoleon

    _____ Duke of Wellington

A. British general who defeated Napoleon at Waterloo

B. English political philosopher who taught that everyone has rights

C. Wrote the Declaration of Independence

D. Great French general who became an all-powerful emperor

E. French king at the time of the French Revolution

F. Known as the Father of the Constitution

G. Revolutionary leader in France who used terror against "enemies of the revolution"

H. Revolutionary War hero and first president of the United States

15. Delegates who met in Philadelphia in 1787 for the Constitutional Convention had a big job to do. They had to write the basic law of government for their new nation. The result of their work was the U.S. Constitution.

Write a paragraph that:

·   Explains what the U.S. Constitution is
·   Names the three branches of government that the U.S. Constitution created
·   Describes at least one power of each branch
·   Explains how the U.S. Constitution keeps any one branch from gaining too much power

A topic sentence is provided, but you should end the paragraph with a concluding sentence.

Delegates met in Philadelphia, Pennsylvania, in 1787 and wrote a new constitution for the United States of America. _____

_____

_____

_____

_____

_____

_____

_____

_____

_____

_____

_____

Student Guide
Lesson 1: Haiti Went First: Toussaint L'Ouverture

Ideas about democracy were not limited to the United States and France. Soon they began to spread throughout most of Latin America. From Haiti to Mexico to Chile, people decided it was time to rule themselves. Revolutions unfolded in country after country. By 1823, the two American continents were filled with republics.

The torch of liberty was burning in France. Now it lit a flame in the French colonies. It began in 1791, in a French colony called Saint Domingue. A former slave led a revolution there. His name was Toussaint L'Ouverture. His followers won independence for the country we know as Haiti.

Lesson Objectives

- Define Latin America.
- Describe the spread of democratic revolution to Latin America.
- Describe Haiti as the first black republic.
- Describe Spain as the major colonial power in Latin America.
- Recognize that a strong class system existed in the Spanish colonies, dividing the population into Spaniards, Creoles, mestizos, Indians, and sometimes slaves.
- Explain that Spain exercised strict control over colonial decisions and that colonists resented their lack of control.
- Locate major colonies-turned-nations on a map of Latin America (Mexico, Venezuela, Colombia, Peru, Bolivia, Argentina, Chile, Brazil).
- Identify key figures and events of major revolutions in Latin America (including Toussaint L'Ouverture, Francisco Miranda, Miguel Hidalgo, Simon Bolívar).
- Describe Saint Domingue as a French colony on the island of Hispaniola and locate it on a map.
- Explain that a large slave population existed on Hispaniola and that the slaves rebelled against their French masters.
- Identify Toussaint L'Ouverture as the leader of the revolution for Haitian independence.
- Describe Haiti as the first black republic.
- Distinguish between weather and climate.
- Describe the relation between latitude and climate.
- Distinguish between polar, temperate, and tropical climates.
- Analyze climate maps for information.

PREPARE

Approximate lesson time is 60 minutes.

Materials

For the Student

📖 Map of Europeans in the New World, 1800

Understanding Geography: Map Skills and Our World (Level 4)

History Journal

Keywords and Pronunciation

climate : The usual pattern of weather in a particular place over a very long period of time.

climate zone : area on earth that has similar temperature, rainfall, snowfall, and sunshine

Haiti (HAY-tee)

Hispaniola (his-puh-NYOH-luh)

revolution (re-vuh-LOO-shuhn) : the traveling of the Earth or another body around the sun; one complete revolution of the earth takes one year

rotation : The spinning of the Earth on its axis; one complete rotation takes one day.

Saint-Domingue (sehn-daw-MEHNG)

Toussaint L'Ouverture (too-SEHN loo-vair-tyour)

weather : The condition of the air at a particular moment of time.

LEARN

Activity 1: L'Ouverture Liberates Haiti *(Online)*

In the French colony of Saint Domingue, on the island of Hispaniola, slaves led a revolt against their French masters. One of their leaders was brave general named Toussaint L'Ouverture.

Activity 2: History Journal *(Offline)*

Instructions

It's time to add another chapter to the story of the past. Follow the directions to complete a new entry in your History Journal.

Turn to a new page in your History Journal. On this page, write a paragraph that tells what the lesson was about. Your work will be used to assess how well you understood the lesson.

Begin with a topic sentence that introduces the paragraph. Include at least three sentences that give details about the lesson. End with a concluding sentence. You may use the Show You Know questions to help you get started.

When you have finished, check your work. Make sure you have written in complete sentences. Check to make sure you used correct capitalization and punctuation. Date your entry and label it with the lesson title.

Guided Learning: Compare your paragraph with the one in the Teacher Guide.

Activity 3: Extra! Extra! Revolution in Haiti! *(Offline)*

Instructions

Follow the instructions to write a short newspaper article about the revolution in Haiti.

Imagine you're a reporter for the *New York Gazette.* You're in Haiti gathering information for an article. Then the revolution begins! Your assignment is to write a short newspaper article on the revolution.

Newspaper articles begin with something called a *lead.* The lead is a short paragraph. It answers most or all of the "five W's and how." The five W's are who, what, where, when, and why. The lead should answer most of these questions. It should also explain how things happened.

There are two reasons to write a lead. One is that it gets the reader's attention. The other is that it helps readers quickly learn the most important facts.

There are several ways to write a lead. Here are some of them:
- Write a sentence or two summing up the whole event.
- Start with a quotation from someone involved in the event.
- Describe the scene where the event took place.
- Ask an interesting question to catch the reader's attention

Use this information to help you write your lead:
- Who: Toussaint L'Ouverture
- What: slave revolt
- Where: colony of St. Domingue on the island of Hispaniola
- When: 1791

Now you find the answers to these two:
- Why?
- How?

Activity 4: Focus on Geography *(Online)*

Instructions

Do you know the difference between weather and climate? To find out:
- Read pages 48–49 of Activity 10, "Weather and Climate," in *Understanding Geography.*
- Answer Questions 1–8 in your History Journal.
- When you have finished, compare your answers with the ones in the Teacher Guide.
- You will be assessed on this geography information after you finish Activity 10 in the next lesson.

ASSESS

Lesson Assessment: Haiti Went First: Toussaint L'Ouverture *(Offline)*

You will complete an online assessment covering the main objectives of this lesson. Your assessment will be scored by the computer.

LEARN
Activity 5. Optional: Haiti Went First: Toussaint L'Ouverture (Offline)
Instructions
What is Haiti like today? Research the country and write a short report.

Do some research on the country of Haiti. Use the Web, the library, and any other good resources you can find. Focus on the Haiti of today.
- Location and geography of Haiti
- Haitian culture (languages, religions, customs, etc.)
- Industry and agriculture of Haiti
- Haiti's climate and weather

Now write a short report. It should include the facts you've learned through your research. Part of your report should be visual. For example, you could include a map, a drawing of Haiti's flag, or a chart showing types of crops grown in Haiti.

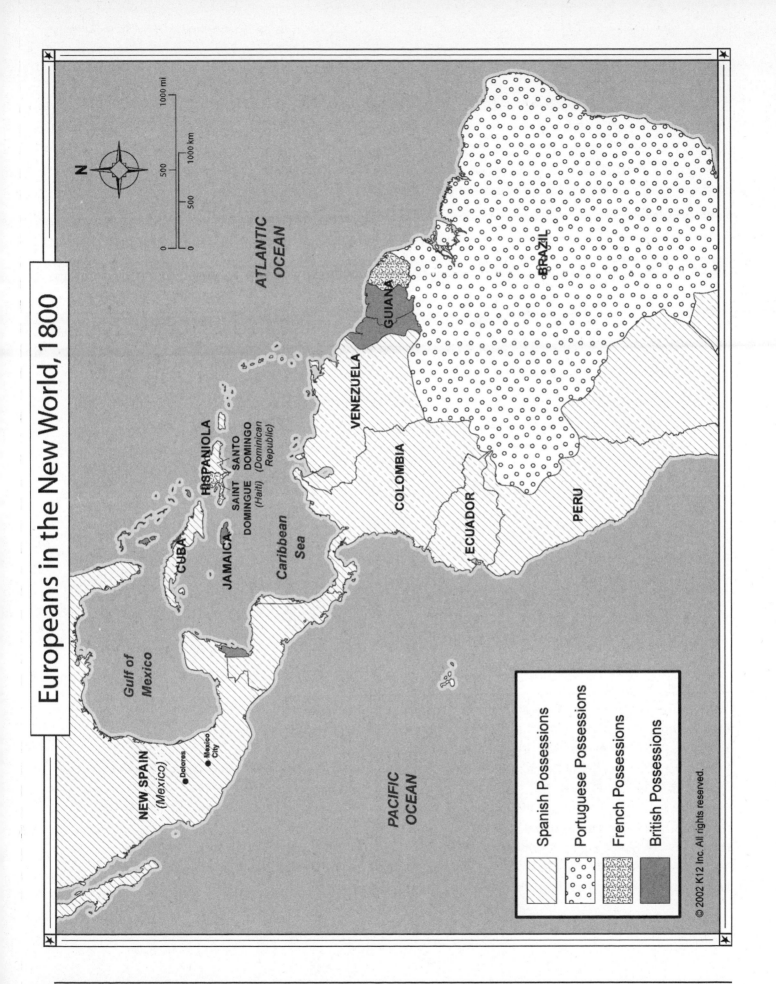

Europeans in the New World, 1800

ATLANTIC OCEAN

BRAZIL

GUIANA

VENEZUELA

COLOMBIA

ECUADOR

PERU

HISPANIOLA
SANTO DOMINGO (Dominican Republic)
SAINT DOMINGUE (Haiti)

CUBA

JAMAICA

Caribbean Sea

Gulf of Mexico

NEW SPAIN (Mexico)

● Dolores ● Mexico City

PACIFIC OCEAN

1000 mi
1000 km
500
500
500
0
0

N

Legend
- Spanish Possessions
- Portuguese Possessions
- French Possessions
- British Possessions

© 2002 K12 Inc. All rights reserved.

Student Guide
Lesson 2: Spanish America and Seeds of Independence

A revolution had unfolded in North America. Another had taken place in France. Now colonists in Latin America took notice. They were part of Spain's vast empire. Spain ruled with a tight fist. "Why shouldn't we be free, too?" Latin American colonists began to ask.

Lesson Objectives

- Explain that in 1800 Spain ruled over most of Central and South America.
- Give one example of ways Spain kept tight control over the colonists (only Spaniards could rule; Spain decided all the American laws).
- Recognize that colonists had come to resent Spain's tight control.
- Explain that some colonists desired independence as they watched events in the young United States and in France.
- Distinguish between weather and climate.
- Describe the relation between latitude and climate.
- Distinguish between polar, temperate, and tropical climates.
- Analyze climate maps for information.
- Explain the relation between seasons in the Northern and Southern Hemispheres.

PREPARE

Approximate lesson time is 60 minutes.

Materials

For the Student

📖 Map of Europeans in the New World, 1800

Understanding Geography: Map Skills and Our World (Level 4)

History Journal

Keywords and Pronunciation

Chile (CHIH-lee)

climate : The usual pattern of weather in a particular place over a very long period of time.

climate zone : area on earth that has similar temperature, rainfall, snowfall, and sunshine

Francisco de Miranda (fran-SEES-koh day mee-RAHN-dah)

Latin America : The area of South, Central, and North America (except for Canada) originally colonized by Spain, Portugal, and France.

revolution (re-vuh-LOO-shuhn) : the traveling of the Earth or another body around the sun; one complete revolution of the earth takes one year

rotation : The spinning of the Earth on its axis; one complete rotation takes one day.

Venezuela (veh-nuh-ZWAY-luh)

weather : The condition of the air at a particular moment of time.

LEARN
Activity 1: Francisco Miranda Recruits *(Online)*

Meet Francisco Miranda, an early Latin American revolutionary, as he recruits soldiers to help him free Venezuela from Spanish rule.

Activity 2: Miranda's Advertisement *(Online)*
Instructions

How did Francisco Miranda get new recruits? Write an advertisement he might have placed in the newspaper.

Activity 3: Focus on Geography *(Online)*
Instructions

Why do we have seasons? To find out:

- Read pages 50–51 of Activity 10, "Weather and Climate," in *Understanding Geography.*
- Answer Questions 9–12 in your History Journal.
- If you have time, you may want to answer the Skill Builder Questions on page 51. They are optional.
- When you have finished, compare your answers with the ones in the Teacher Guide.

ASSESS

Lesson Assessment: Spanish America and Seeds of Independence, Part 1
(*Online*)

You will complete an online assessment covering the main objectives of this lesson. Your assessment will be scored by the computer.

Lesson Assessment: Spanish America and Seeds of Independence, Part 2
(*Offline*)

Have an adult review your essay and input the results in the assessment at the end of the lesson.

LEARN
Activity 4: Spanish America and Seeds of Independence *(Online)*
Instructions

How creative are you? Test your creativity by creating a project about the seasons. Follow the directions in the Try It Yourself section on page 51.

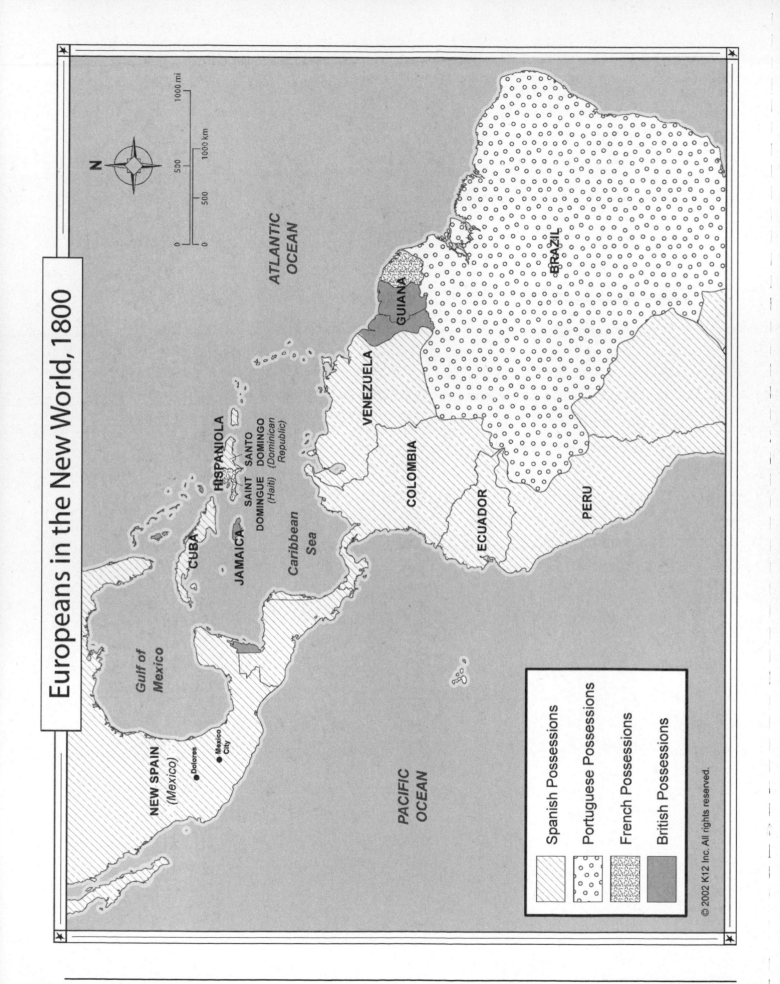

Europeans in the New World, 1800

ATLANTIC OCEAN

BRAZIL

GUIANA

VENEZUELA

COLOMBIA

ECUADOR

PERU

HISPANIOLA

SANTO DOMINGO *(Dominican Republic)*

SAINT DOMINGUE *(Haiti)*

JAMAICA

CUBA

Caribbean Sea

Gulf of Mexico

NEW SPAIN *(Mexico)*

Mexico City

Dolores

PACIFIC OCEAN

1000 mi

1000 km

500

500

0

0

N

Spanish Possessions

Portuguese Possessions

French Possessions

British Possessions

Lesson Assessment

Spanish America and Seeds of Independence, Part 2

How did Francisco Miranda get new recruits? Write an advertisement he might have placed in the newspaper.

Student Guide
Lesson 3: Miguel Hidalgo: Father of Mexican Independence

Napoleon had invaded Spain. And the news had reached the colonists in Spanish America. Now they thought of their own futures. They wondered if the time had come to rule themselves. One was a priest named Father Miguel Hidalgo. He rallied many people in Mexico. They started the Mexican war for independence.

Lesson Objectives

- Identify Miguel Hidalgo as a Mexican priest and the Father of Mexican Independence.
- Explain that Miguel Hidalgo called the people of Hidalgo's church together and urged them to rebel against Spain.
- State that Hidalgo's famous speech (*Grito de Dolores*) is read every year on Mexican Independence Day.
- Define and give examples of precipitation.
- Describe rain forests and deserts in terms of precipitation.
- Analyze precipitation maps and graphs for information on climate.

PREPARE

Approximate lesson time is 60 minutes.

Materials

For the Student

📖 Map of Europeans in the New World, 1800

Understanding Geography: Map Skills and Our World (Level 4)

History Journal

Keywords and Pronunciation

climograph : a special kind of graph that shows the average temperature and precipitation in a certain place during a year

creoles (KREE-ohls) : In the context of this lesson, people of Spanish descent who were born in the Spanish American colonies.

Dolores (doh-LOH-res)

eucalyp : A dry, often sandy area that gets very little rain.

Francisco de Miranda (fran-SEES-koh day mee-RAHN-dah)

Grito de Dolores (GREE-toh day doh-LOH-res)

mestizos (meh-STEE-zohs) : People with both Indian and Spanish ancestors.

Miguel Hidalgo (mee-GEHL ee-DAHL-goh)

precipitation : The moisture that falls to the Earth; rain, snow, sleet, and hail are all forms of precipitation.

rain forest : A densely wooded area that receives more than 100 inches of rain per year.

LEARN
Activity 1: The Cry of Dolores *(Online)*
Learn how Miguel Hidalgo's speech in the town of Dolores began the fight for Mexican independence.

Activity 2: History Journal *(Online)*
Instructions
It's time to add another chapter to the story of our past. Create a new entry in your History Journal.

Activity 3: Grito de Dolores *(Online)*
Instructions
Write a speech that Father Hidalgo might have given in Dolores.

Activity 4: Focus on Geography *(Online)*
Instructions
What's the most significant difference between a desert and a rain forest? Rain. The amount of moisture an area receives determines what plants grow there. To learn more about climate and precipitation maps:

- Read pages 52– 53 of Activity 11, "Climate and Precipitation," in *Understanding Geography.*
- Answer Questions 1–7 in your History Journal.
- When you have finished, compare your answers with the ones in the Teacher Guide.
- You will be assessed on this geography information after you finish Activity 11 in the next lesson.

ASSESS

Lesson Assessment: Miguel Hidalgo: Father of Mexican Independence
(Online)
You will complete an online assessment covering the main objectives of this lesson. Your assessment will be scored by the computer.

LEARN
Activity 5. Optional: Miguel Hidalgo: Father of Mexican Independence *(Online)*

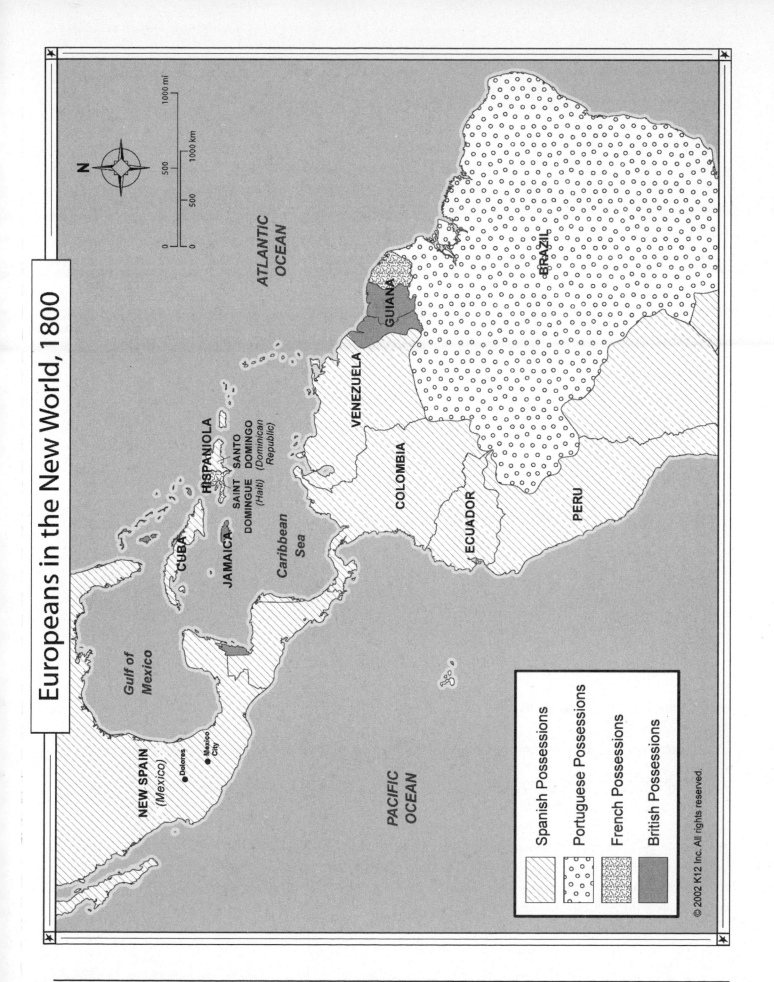

Europeans in the New World, 1800

ATLANTIC OCEAN

PACIFIC OCEAN

Gulf of Mexico

Caribbean Sea

NEW SPAIN (Mexico)

Mexico City

Dolores

CUBA

JAMAICA

HISPANIOLA

SAINT DOMINGUE (Haiti)

SANTO DOMINGO (Dominican Republic)

BRAZIL

GUIANA

VENEZUELA

COLOMBIA

ECUADOR

PERU

1000 mi

1000 km

500

500

500

0

0

N

Spanish Possessions

Portuguese Possessions

French Possessions

British Possessions

Student Guide
Lesson 4: Simón Bolívar: The Liberator

The revolutions in the United States and France inspired a new leader. Simón Bolívar led the fight for Spanish American independence. He freed his own country, Venezuela, from Spanish rule. Then he marched on. He marched into Colombia. He marched into Ecuador and Peru. He marched into Bolivia, the country that took his name. In much of South America, he is called "the Liberator."

Lesson Objectives

- Describe Simón Bolívar as a great South American revolutionary and general.
- Explain that Bolívar led military campaigns to free much of Spanish America and is known as "the Liberator."
- Name at least two areas that Bolívar liberated.
- Locate the areas Bolívar liberated (Venezuela, Colombia, Panama, Ecuador, Peru, and Bolivia) on a map of South America.
- Identify Bolivia as a country named for Bolívar.
- Define and give examples of precipitation.
- Describe rain forests and deserts in terms of precipitation.
- Analyze precipitation maps and graphs for information on climate.
- Use climographs to gain information.

PREPARE

Approximate lesson time is 60 minutes.

Materials

For the Student

- Map of South America (Gran Colombia)
- The Liberation of South America

Understanding Geography: Map Skills and Our World (Level 4)

History Journal

Keywords and Pronunciation

Caracas (kah-RAH-kahs)

climograph : a special kind of graph that shows the average temperature and precipitation in a certain place during a year

Creole (KREE-ohl) : In the context of this lesson, people of Spanish descent who were born in the Spanish-American colonies.

eucalyp : A dry, often sandy area that gets very little rain.

liberate : In the context of this lesson, to free from the control of a foreign power.

precipitation : The moisture that falls to the Earth; rain, snow, sleet, and hail are all forms of precipitation.

rain forest : A densely wooded area that receives more than 100 inches of rain per year.

Simón Bolívar (see-MOHN buh-LEE-vahr)

Venezuela (veh-nuh-ZWAY-luh)

LEARN
Activity 1: Bolívar Liberates South America *(Online)*
Meet Simón Bolívar, the man who liberated much of South America from Spanish rule.

Activity 2: History Journal *(Online)*

Activity 3: The Liberation of South America *(Offline)*
Instructions
Simón Bolívar's military campaigns freed much of South America from Spanish rule. Complete Part 1 of the Liberation of South America activity sheet to trace his path of revolution.
Save this activity sheet. You will complete Part 2 in the next lesson.

Activity 4: Focus on Geography *(Online)*
Instructions
To learn more about climographs and the climate of Africa:
- Read pages 54– 55 of Activity 11, "Climate and Precipitation," in *Understanding Geography*.
- Answer Questions 8–16 in your History Journal.
- When you have finished, compare your answers with the ones in the Teacher Guide.

ASSESS
Lesson Assessment: Simón Bolívar: The Liberator, Part 1 *(Online)*
You will complete an online assessment covering the main objectives of this lesson. Your assessment will be scored by the computer.

Lesson Assessment: Simon Bolivar - The Liberator, Part 2 *(Offline)*
Have an adult review your answers to the Show You Know: History Journal activity, and input the results online.

LEARN
Activity 5. Optional: Simon Bolivar: The Liberator *(Online)*

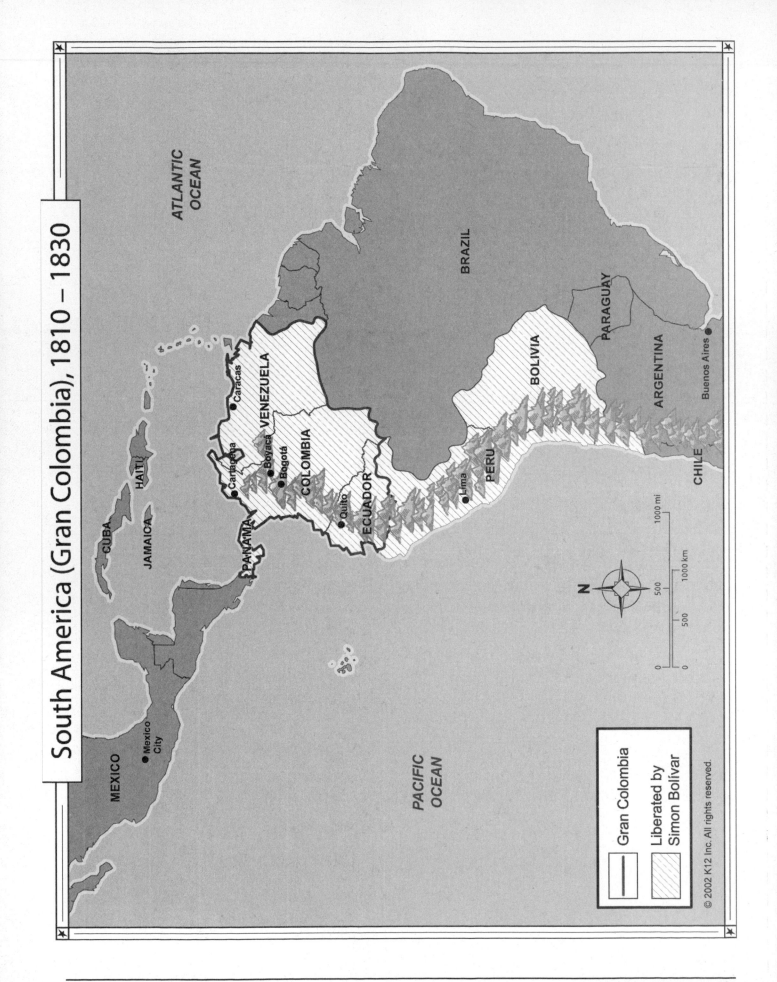

South America (Gran Colombia), 1810 – 1830

ATLANTIC OCEAN

PACIFIC OCEAN

MEXICO
Mexico City

CUBA

HAITI

JAMAICA

PANAMA

Cartagena

Caracas

VENEZUELA

Boyacá

Bogotá

COLOMBIA

Quito

ECUADOR

PERU

Lima

BOLIVIA

BRAZIL

PARAGUAY

ARGENTINA

CHILE

Buenos Aires

N

1000 mi

1000 km

500

500

Gran Colombia

Liberated by Simon Bolívar

Name _____ Date _____

The Liberation of South America

Part 1

1. On the map, write "1" on the first country Bolívar liberated. Then label the country by writing its name on the line provided.

2. Starting from the first country, draw a solid black line with an arrow. It should point to the country he marched to and liberated next. Write "2" and the name of that country on the line.

3. Draw an arrow from the second country to the third country Bolívar liberated. Write "3" and the country's name on the line.

4. From the third country, draw an arrow to the fourth country he and his forces liberated. Write "4" and the country's name on the line.

5. These four smaller countries formed a new, independent country. What was its name? _____

6. Who was elected president of this new country? _____

7. Draw an arrow from the fourth country to the fifth country Bolívar liberated. Write "5" and the country's name on the line.

8. Bolívar turned a section of the fifth country into a separate country. Write "6" and this country's name on the line provided. (Hint: The country named itself to honor Bolívar.)

The Liberation of South America

The Liberation of South America

Part 2: Complete after the Liberating the South: San Martín and O'Higgins lesson.

1. Show the Andes mountain range on the map using this symbol: ^. Add this symbol to the map legend.

2. What two South American leaders combined forces to defeat the Spanish?

    _____

    _____

3. On the map, write "7" and label the country where the Army of the Andes began its march.

4. Write "8" and label the country that the Army of the Andes marched to and liberated.

Lesson Assessment

Simón Bolívar: The Liberator, Part 2

1. Describe Simón Bolívar. _____

2. What is Bolívar known as? _____

3. What did he do? _____

4. Name at least two areas that Bolívar liberated (freed). _____

5. What country was named for Simón Bolívar? _____

Student Guide
Lesson 5. Optional: Liberating the South: San Martín and O'Higgins

In South America, two men joined forces to liberate their countries. José de San Martín came from Argentina. Bernardo O'Higgins came from Chile. San Martín led the fight for Argentina's independence. Then he joined forces with O'Higgins. Their army crossed the Andes in 1817. They freed Chile from Spanish rule. Then they helped Bolívar liberate Peru.

Lesson Objectives

- Identify José de San Martín and Bernardo O'Higgins as two great liberators of South America.
- Locate the Andes on a map.
- Describe the Army of the Andes as forces led by San Martín and O'Higgins that crossed the Andes mountain range.
- Explain that San Martín and O'Higgins liberated Chile.

PREPARE

Approximate lesson time is 60 minutes.

Materials

For the Student

   📖 Map of South America, 1810 -1830

   map, world

   📖 The Liberation of South America

Keywords and Pronunciation

Andes (AN-deez)

Buenos Aires (BWAY-nuhs AIR-eez)

Ecuador (EH-kwuh-dor)

José de San Martín (hoh-SAY day san mahr-TEEN)

La Plata (lah PLAH-tah)

Lima (LEE-muh)

Paraguay (pah-rah-GWIY)

Uruguay (oo-roo-GWIY)

LEARN
Activity 1. Optional: Optional Lesson Instructions *(Online)*

Activity 2. Optional: San Martín and O'Higgins Team Up *(Online)*

Argentina and Chile joined the fight for independence from Spain. Read about how José de San Martín and Bernardo O'Higgins teamed up to liberate South America's southern cone.

Activity 3. Optional: History Journal *(Offline)*

Instructions

It's time to add another chapter to the story of our past. Create a new entry in your History Journal.

Turn to a new page in your History Journal. On this page, write a paragraph that tells what the lesson was about.

Begin with a topic sentence that introduces the paragraph. Include at least three sentences that give details about the lesson. End with a concluding sentence. You may use the Show You Know questions to help you get started.

When you have finished, check your work. Make sure you have written in complete sentences. Check to make sure you used correct capitalization and punctuation. Date your entry and label it with the lesson title.

Guided Learning: Compare your paragraph with the one in the Teacher Guide.

Activity 4. Optional: The Liberation of South America *(Online)*

Instructions

Bolívar was not the only one in South America fighting for freedom from Spain. Two other men from South America teamed up to fight the Spanish.

Take out the Liberation of South America activity sheet that you started in the last lesson. (If you don't have it, print another copy.) Complete Part 2.

Activity 5. Optional: Liberating the South: San Martin and O'Higgins *(Offline)*

Instructions

How do the Andes stack up against other mountain ranges? Do some research to find out.

The march of the Army of the Andes is one of the most famous military marches in history. The main reason for this is that the army crossed some of the highest mountains in the world--the Andes. They traveled through mountain passes almost 13,000 feet high.

There are other mountain ranges with mountains as high as those in the Andes, or even higher. Do some research on the Andes and two other mountain ranges. Then create a chart on poster board or construction paper. It should show information about the three mountain ranges.

You could include some or all of these facts in your chart:
- the location (continent) of the mountain range
- the name of the tallest peak in the range
- the length of the range
- an interesting historical fact about the range
- the names of people who climbed or explored it

The Liberation of South America

PACIFIC
OCEAN

Cartagena

Caracas

Bogotá

Quito

Amazon River

Lima

ATLANTIC
OCEAN

Buenos Aires
La Plata

Rio de
la Plata

N

| 0 | 500 | 1000 mi |
| 0 | 500 | 1000 km |

Name _____   Date _____

The Liberation of South America

Part 1

1. On the map, write "1" on the first country Bolívar liberated. Then label the country by writing its name on the line provided.

2. Starting from the first country, draw a solid black line with an arrow. It should point to the country he marched to and liberated next. Write "2" and the name of that country on the line.

3. Draw an arrow from the second country to the third country Bolívar liberated. Write "3" and the country's name on the line.

4. From the third country, draw an arrow to the fourth country he and his forces liberated. Write "4" and the country's name on the line.

5. These four smaller countries formed a new, independent country. What was its name? _____

6. Who was elected president of this new country? _____

7. Draw an arrow from the fourth country to the fifth country Bolívar liberated. Write "5" and the country's name on the line.

8. Bolívar turned a section of the fifth country into a separate country. Write "6" and this country's name on the line provided. (Hint: The country named itself to honor Bolívar.)

The Liberation of South America

Part 2: Complete after the Liberating the South: San Martín and O'Higgins lesson.

1. Show the Andes mountain range on the map using this symbol: ^. Add this symbol to the map legend.

2. What two South American leaders combined forces to defeat the Spanish?

    _____

    _____

3. On the map, write "7" and label the country where the Army of the Andes began its march.

4. Write "8" and label the country that the Army of the Andes marched to and liberated.

South America, 1810 – 1830

ATLANTIC OCEAN

PANAMA

● Cartagena

● Caracas

VENEZUELA

BRITISH
DUTCH
FRENCH

GUIANA

● Bogotá

COLOMBIA

● Quito

ECUADOR

Amazon River

Andes

● Lima

PERU

BRAZIL

BOLIVIA

Andes

PARAGUAY

PACIFIC OCEAN

ARGENTINA

URUGUAY

Buenos Aires ●
La Plata

Rio de la Plata

ATLANTIC OCEAN

CHILE

N

| 0 | 500 | 1000 mi |
| 0 | 500 | 1000 km |

| —— | La Plata |

Student Guide
Lesson 6: Unit Review and Assessment

You've completed this unit, and now it's time to review what you've learned and take the unit assessment.

Lesson Objectives

- Demonstrate mastery of important knowledge and skills in this unit.
- Demonstrate mastery of important knowledge and skills taught in previous lessons.
- Identify Toussaint L'Ouverture as the leader of the revolution for Haitian independence.
- Give one example of ways Spain kept tight control over the colonists (only Spaniards could rule; Spain decided all the American laws).
- Recognize that colonists had come to resent Spain's tight control.
- Explain that some colonists desired independence as they watched events in the young United States and in France.
- Identify Miguel Hidalgo as a Mexican priest and the Father of Mexican Independence.
- Explain that Bolívar led military campaigns to free much of Spanish America and is known as "the Liberator."
- Locate the areas Bolívar liberated (Venezuela, Colombia, Panama, Ecuador, Peru, and Bolivia) on a map of South America.
- Define Latin America.
- Describe Haiti as the first black republic.
- Describe Spain as the major colonial power in Latin America.
- Recognize that a strong class system existed in the Spanish colonies, dividing the population into Spaniards, Creoles, mestizos, Indians, and sometimes slaves.
- Explain that Spain exercised strict control over colonial decisions and that colonists resented their lack of control.

PREPARE

Approximate lesson time is 60 minutes.

LEARN
Activity 1: Latin American Revolutions (Offline)

Instructions

We've covered a lot, and now it's time to take a look back. Here's what you should remember about Latin American revolutions.

You'll need the following maps from your History Journal: Europeans in the New World, 1800; South America (Gran Colombia), 1810-1830.

Powerful kings and queens ruled through much of history. But human beings are creatures who want to rule themselves. We want to control our own future. The Greeks understood that. They gave us democracy. The Romans understood that. They created a republic. The English understood that. They gave us the Magna Carta.

In 1776, Americans understood people's need to rule themselves. In 1789, the French did, too. Such ideas can spread quickly. By 1823, they had spread throughout most of Latin America.

The wars for independence in Latin America spanned a whole continent and more. Let's walk through the ones we've studied. We'll look at our map and play "What do we know?"

Look at the Caribbean Sea and find Hispaniola. What is the name of the western half of that island? [1]

Haiti was home to the first Latin American revolution for independence. The year was 1791. Who led that revolution? [2]

Which country did Toussaint and his fellow Haitians rebel against? [3]

What kind of life had L'Ouverture led before the revolution? [4]

The revolution on Haiti was unusual. It was not just a revolution for independence. It was a revolution for freedom from slavery. Black slaves rebelled against their French masters and won. Haiti became the first black republic.

Now look south. Find Venezuela. A man from Venezuela named Francisco Miranda traveled to France in the 1790s. He traveled to the United States, too. He was in love with ideas about freedom. He wanted George Washington and John Adams to help the people of South America gain their freedom. What country ruled most of the colonies in Central and South America? [5]

How did people born in Spain treat the Creoles or Spanish Americans in those colonies? [6]

Why did Miranda want Spanish America to be free of Spain? [7]

In time, many other Spanish Americans came to agree with Miranda. "It's time to rule ourselves," they said. That idea spread. Then Napoleon marched into Spain. He put his brother on the throne. When that happened, revolutions started in Spanish America. The people there did not want to be ruled by a Frenchman! Even after Napoleon was overthrown, Spanish Americans still wanted to be free.

Now find Mexico on your map. Mexico was called "New Spain." It was one of the first colonies the Spanish settled. Spanish, Creoles, mestizos, and Indians now lived side by side, but not happily. Do you remember the name of the priest who started the revolution in Mexico? [8]

Father Hidalgo was angry about the way people from Spain treated the Creoles, mestizos, and Indians. He gave a great speech calling on the Indians and mestizos to rise up against Spain. They did. After many bloody years of war, Mexico won independence.

Now let's move southeast. Find the countries of Venezuela, Colombia, Ecuador, and Bolivia. One man led the independence forces in these great nations. What was his name? (Hint: The country of Bolivia was named after him.) [9]

Like Miranda, Bolívar had studied in Europe. He turned out to be one of the most determined liberators of all time. He freed his homeland of Venezuela. Then he marched on to Colombia. He yanked Ecuador and the land that is now Bolivia away from Spain.

While Bolívar was fighting for independence in the north, others were fighting in the south. José de San Martín led the movement for independence in a large country east of the Andes mountain range. What is that country called? [10]

San Martín had also studied in Europe. He had been a soldier in Spain. But he was tired of Argentina being under the heavy boot of Spain. After he freed Argentina, he wanted to make sure his country was safe.

Then a fellow from across the Andes came to talk to San Martín. This fellow wanted help liberating the land on the western side of the mountains. San Martín said he would help. Which long, skinny country is on the western side of the Andes mountain range? [11]

What was the name of the man from Chile who wanted to team up with San Martín to defeat the Spanish? [12]

This bold fight for independence from Spain began with a famous mountain trek. In Argentina, San Martín and O'Higgins organized the Army of the Andes. They gathered thousands of men and hundreds of horses. They led their army through high mountain passes. The Army of the Andes surprised the Spanish on the other side. Leading the fighting in Chile, O'Higgins and San Martín won the day.

After Chile, just one big country remained to be liberated in Spanish America. What was it? (Hint: It had been home to the Incas before the Spanish came.) [13]

Two great Spanish American liberators, Simón Bolívar and José de San Martín, went after the Spanish army in Peru. Bolívar came from the north and camped outside Lima. San Martín and his navy approached from the south. They both closed in on Lima. They freed Peru and captured the hearts of its people.

Look again at the map of South America. We have covered just about all of it--except for one big country. Which big country have we left out in our study of wars for independence? [14]

The colony of Brazil did not belong to Spain. It belonged to Portugal. We did not study Brazil in these lessons because Brazil did not have a revolution for independence at this time.

In fact, at this time Brazil became home to the Portuguese king and queen! That's right. When Napoleon conquered Spain, he invaded Portugal, too. The Portuguese king and queen didn't sit around waiting to be tossed in jail. They got on a ship and headed for their favorite colony--Brazil. The Portuguese king and queen found a home there. So Brazil stayed loyal. This one kingdom alone continued to exist in the Americas, which were now two continents filled with republics.

Activity 2: History Journal Review *(Offline)*

Instructions

It's time to prepare for the unit assessment by reviewing your History Journal.

Use your History Journal to review the unit called Latin American Revolutions. Take some time to go over the work you've done. An adult can also help you review by asking you questions based on the work in your journal.

Activity 3: Online Interactive Review *(Online)*

ASSESS

Unit Assessment: Latin American Revolutions (*Offline*)

Complete an offline Unit Assessment. Your learning coach will score this part of the Assessment.

Name _____ Date _____

Latin American Revolutions

Read each question and its answer choices. Fill in the bubble in front of the word or words that best answer each question.

Questions marked with an asterisk (*) have more than one correct answer. For these questions, fill in the bubble next to *all* correct answers.

1. Which Latin American nation became the first black republic?

   ⓐ   Cuba

   ⓑ   Haiti

   ⓒ   Panama

   ⓓ   Colombia

2. One European country had colonies in most of South America. Which country was it?

   ⓐ   England

   ⓑ   Spain

   ⓒ   Portugal

   ⓓ   France

3. Which of the following best describes how Spain ruled its South American colonies?

   ⓐ   Spain selected Creoles to govern the colonies.

   ⓑ   Spain allowed most decisions to be made by the colonists.

   ⓒ   Spain kept tight control over the colonies.

   ⓓ   Spain shared control equally with the colonists.

4. "I was a slave on the French colony of Saint Domingue. I led a revolution and helped found the new nation of Haiti. Who am I?"

   (a) Miguel Hidalgo

   (b) Bernardo O'Higgins

   (c) Toussaint L'Ouverture

   (d) Francisco Miranda

5. A person from which of the following groups could rule a Spanish colony in South America?

   (a) Indians

   (b) mestizos

   (c) Creoles

   (d) Spaniards

6. Latin America includes _____.

   (a) all of North America and part of South America

   (b) all of Central America and all of North America

   (c) part of North America, and all of Central and South America

   (d) part of Central America, and all of North and South America

7. "I was a great South American revolutionary and general. I led military campaigns to free much of Spanish America. I was known as 'the Liberator.' Who am I?"

   (a) Simón Bolívar

   (b) Miquel Hidalgo

   (c) Francisco Miranda

   (d) José de San Martín

8. Democratic revolutions in two countries inspired many colonists in Spanish America to seek independence. Which two countries?

   (a) France and Holland

   (b) United States and France

   (c) Spain and Portugal

   (d) England and Scotland

9. "I was a Mexican priest. I gave a speech urging my people to rebel against Spain. I am known as the Father of Mexican Independence. Who am I?"

   (a) Miguel Hidalgo

   (b) José de San Martín

   (c) Simón Bolívar

   (d) Toussaint L'Ouverture

10. There were Creoles, mestizos, Indians, slaves, and Spaniards in South America. Those groups show that Spanish American colonies had _____.

   (a) a new way of organizing government

   (b) a strong class system based on birth

   (c) settlers from many parts of Europe

   (d) a large number of people making decisions

11. What did Creoles think about Spanish rule?

ⓐ They admired Spanish rule and were happy not to have the task of governing themselves.

ⓑ They resented Spanish control and wanted colonists to make more decisions.

ⓒ They were proud to be Spanish and pleased with their heritage of liberty.

ⓓ They were angry that Spaniards gave too much power to mestizos.

*12. Latin America was originally colonized by which of the following countries? (Select *all* that are correct.)

ⓐ Germany

ⓑ France

ⓒ Spain

ⓓ Portugal

ⓔ Italy

13. On the map, label these nations that won their independence
from Spain and Portugal.

Mexico	Colombia	Bolivia	Brazil
Venezuela	Peru		

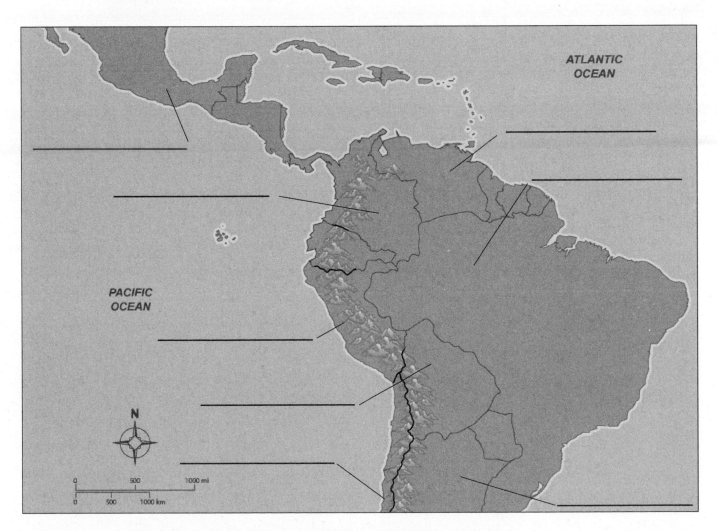

Extra Challenge: Also label Chile and Argentina.

Student Guide
Lesson 1: James Hargreaves and the Spinning Jenny

It started in Great Britain around 1750 and quickly spread to mainland Europe and America. Steam engines hissed and roared. New machines made all kinds of things. Factories sprang up. People flocked to cities. Steamboats, trains, and better roads carried people just about everywhere. We call this the Industrial Revolution, and it changed the world forever.

The Industrial Revolution began in the late eighteenth century. It began in Great Britain. And it changed the way people worked and lived. Now far more goods could be produced. Advances in the textile industry sparked these changes. James Hargreaves invented the spinning jenny. It made Britain a leader in cloth production.

Lesson Objectives

- Describe the Industrial Revolution as a time when more and more goods were produced by power-driven machinery.
- Explain that the Industrial Revolution began in England.
- Explain that during the Industrial Revolution production moved out of the home and into factories.
- Name some improvements in transportation that took place during the Industrial Revolution.
- Explain that in the early stages of the Industrial Revolution working conditions were harsh and workers suffered.
- Identify important figures, inventions, and ideas of the Industrial Revolution (James Watt, Robert Fulton, Charles Dickens, Karl Marx, spinning jenny, steam engine, steamboat, railroads, capitalism, Marxism).
- Explain that the Industrial Revolution was a change in the way people lived and produced things, and that it started in Great Britain.
- Recognize that many of the first innovations of the Industrial Revolution were in the textile industry.
- Identify James Hargreaves as the inventor of the spinning jenny.
- Describe the spinning jenny as a machine that spun many threads together and greatly increased the amount of thread available for weaving.
- Review important geographic knowledge and skills.

PREPARE

Approximate lesson time is 60 minutes.

Materials

For the Student

Understanding Geography: Map Skills and Our World (Level 4)

Keywords and Pronunciation

loom : A frame or machine that weavers use to weave thread into cloth.

spindle : A round stick used to make thread while spinning.

spinning wheel : A machine for spinning thread.

LEARN
Activity 1: The Beginning of the Industrial Revolution (Online)

Activity 2: History Journal (Online)
Instructions
It's time to add another chapter to the story of our past. Create a new entry in your History Journal.

Activity 3: Presenting the James Hargreaves Exhibit (Online)
Instructions
Pretend you're a tour guide at a museum. What will you tell visitors about James Hargreaves and the spinning jenny?

Activity 4: Geography Review (Online)
Instructions
It's time to look back and review some of the geography skills you've learned before you take the assessment in the next lesson.

- Begin reviewing by clicking the online Geography Review.
- When you have finished the online review, go back to the Skill Builders in *Understanding Geography* Activities 1–12 and answer one question from each activity.
- If you have time, you may wish to answer the Map Review questions on pages 60–61 of *Understanding Geography*. They are optional. When you have finished, compare your answers to the ones in the Teacher Guide.

ASSESS

Lesson Assessment: James Hargreaves and the Spinning Jenny (*Online*)
You will complete an online assessment covering the main objectives of this lesson. Your assessment will be scored by the computer.

LEARN
Activity 5. Optional: James Hargreaves and the Spinning Jenny (Online)
How did people spin thread before they had spinning wheels? Find out in this activity.

Student Guide
Lesson 2: James Watt and the Steam Engine

Early industry used animals, water, and human muscle. Then steam became a source of power. James Watt designed a new steam engine. There had been steam engines before. But this one was much more efficient. Now factories could use power-driven machinery. And the Industrial Revolution got a huge boost.

Lesson Objectives

- Explain that before the Industrial Revolution, people relied on animals, water, and their own muscles for power.
- Describe steam engines as important in the Industrial Revolution because they supplied much more power.
- Identify James Watt as a Scottish engineer who designed an efficient steam engine.
- Recognize that Watt's steam engine could be used to power many machines.
- Demonstrate mastery of important geographic knowledge and skills.

PREPARE

Approximate lesson time is 60 minutes.

Materials

For the Student

paper, 8 1/2" x 11"

pencils, colored, 16 colors or more

Keywords and Pronunciation

Erasmus Darwin (ih-RAZ-muhs DAHR-wuhn)

lunatic : A crazy person.

LEARN
Activity 1: A Full Head of Steam (Online)

Activity 2: History Journal (Offline)

Instructions

It's time to add another chapter to the story of the past. Follow the directions to complete a new entry in your History Journal.

Turn to a new page in your History Journal and complete the paragraph that follows. Use the words from the word list to help you. Be careful, though. There are more words than you need. And two choices are used more than once.

Before the _____ took place, people had to use _____, _____, or their own strength to run _____. Then _____, a Scottish engineer, invented a new and efficient _____. It did not use too much fuel. The _____ was important because it could supply a lot of _____. People used this invention to run boats, trains, looms, and many other _____.

Word List:

animals

steam

lightning

Industrial Revolution

James Fulton

James Watt

cloth

Machine Age

machines

power

steam engine

steam iron

water

Guided Learning: When you have finished, have an adult check your work. Date your entry and label it with the lesson title.

Activity 3: Buy a Steam Engine! *(Offline)*

Instructions

People will want to buy Watt's fabulous new invention. Tell them why!

Create an advertisement for James Watt's new steam engine. You'll want to teach people about the engine. And, of course, you'll want to persuade them to buy it. Before you begin, look at some examples of ads in newspapers, magazines, or other sources. Be sure you highlight all the key features of this marvelous machine.

Activity 4. Optional: James Watt and the Steam Engine *(Online)*

ASSESS

Lesson Assessment: James Watt and the Steam Engine, Part 1 (*Online*)

You will complete an online assessment covering the main objectives of this lesson. Your assessment will be scored by the computer.

Lesson Assessment: James Watt and the Steam Engine, Part 2 (*Offline*)

You will complete an offline assessment covering the main objectives of this lesson. Your learning coach will score this assessment.

Lesson Assessment

James Watt and the Steam Engine, Part 2

1. **Teacher / Learning Coach: Please refer to your student's answers in the History Journal Activity for this question.**

   Turn to a new page in your History Journal and complete the paragraph that follows. Use the words from the word list to help you. Be careful, though. There are more words than you need. And two choices are used more than once.

animals
steam
lightning
Industrial Revolution
James Fulton
James Watt
cloth
Machine Age
machines
power
steam engine
steam iron
water

   Before the _____ took place, people had to use _____, _____, or their own strength to run _____. Then _____, a Scottish engineer, invented a new and efficient _____. It did not use too much fuel. The _____ was important because it could supply a lot of _____. People used this invention to run boats, trains, looms, and many other _____.

2. Label each Location on the map.

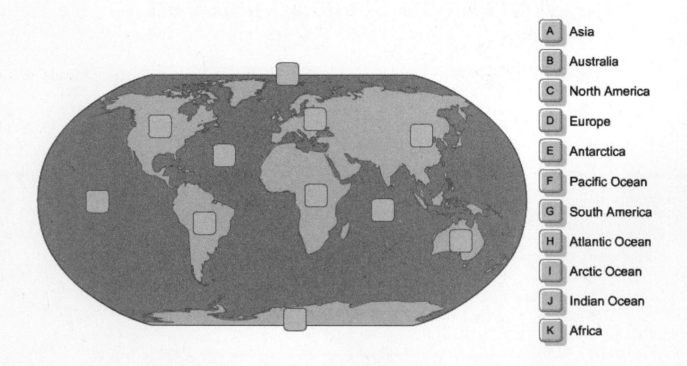

A	Asia
B	Australia
C	North America
D	Europe
E	Antarctica
F	Pacific Ocean
G	South America
H	Atlantic Ocean
I	Arctic Ocean
J	Indian Ocean
K	Africa

Student Guide
Lesson 3: Fulton and McAdam: A Revolution in Transportation

The steam engine had created a new source of power. Now the Industrial Revolution sped forward. Two new inventions made it faster to move people and goods from place to place. In America, Robert Fulton invented the first practical steamboat. In Britain, John Loudon McAdam worked on improving roads. His macadam pavement made it faster and easier to travel by land.

Lesson Objectives

- List the steamboat and better roads as major improvements in transportation.
- Identify Robert Fulton as the inventor of the first practical steamboat.
- Identify John McAdam as a man who improved the paving of roads.

PREPARE

Approximate lesson time is 60 minutes.

Keywords and Pronunciation

macadamized (muh-KA-duh-miyzd)

LEARN
Activity 1: Many Roads to Travel *(Online)*

Activity 2: History Journal *(Offline)*

Instructions

It's time to add another chapter to the story of the past. Follow the directions to complete a new entry in your History Journal.

Turn to a new page in your History Journal. On this page, write a paragraph that tells what the lesson was about. Begin with a topic sentence that introduces the paragraph. Include at least three sentences that give details about the lesson. End with a concluding sentence. You may use the Show You Know questions to help you get started.

When you have finished, check your work. Make sure you have written in complete sentences. Check to make sure you used correct capitalization and punctuation. Date your entry and label it with the lesson title.

Guided Learning: Compare your paragraph with the one in the Teacher Guide.

Activity 3: Your Choice of Transportation? *(Online)*

ASSESS
Lesson Assessment: Fulton and McAdam: A Revolution in Transportation
(Online)

You will complete an offline assessment covering the main objectives of this lesson. Your learning coach will score this assessment.

LEARN
Activity 4. Optional: Fulton and McAdam: A Revolution in Transportation *(Online)*

Name _____   Date _____

Lesson Assessment

Fulton and McAdam: A Revolution in Transportation

1. Improving canals made water transportation better. In this lesson, you learned about two other big

   improvements in transportation. What were they?_____

2. Who built the first practical steamboat? _____

3. Who invented a better kind of road surface? _____

Student Guide
Lesson 4: Americans Climb Aboard

Steamboats made it easier to move people and things by water. Better roads improved travel by land. But it was the railroad that really made things go a mile a minute.

Lesson Objectives

- Explain that the Industrial Revolution included a revolution in transportation.
- Explain that the steam-powered locomotive made it possible to move people and goods quickly over great distances.
- Explain that Americans used the railroad to connect the country from the Atlantic to the Pacific Ocean.

PREPARE

Approximate lesson time is 60 minutes.

Materials

> For the Student
>> Inventors: A Library of Congress Book by Martin Sandler
>>
>> map, U.S.
>>
>> 🖳 From Sea to Shining Sea activity sheet
>>
>> Building the Transcontinental Railroad by Monica Halpern

LEARN
Activity 1: All Aboard: America Rides the Rails *(Online)*

By the end of the 1800s, half the world's railway track lay in the United States. Learn about the inventors and inventions that made this possible.

Activity 2: History Journal *(Offline)*
Instructions

It's time to add another chapter to the story of the past. Follow the directions to complete a new entry in your History Journal.

Turn to a new page in your History Journal. On this page, write a paragraph that tells what the lesson was about.

Begin with a topic sentence that introduces the paragraph. Include at least three sentences that give details about the lesson. End with a concluding sentence. You may use the Show You Know questions to help you get started.

When you have finished, check your work. Make sure you have written in complete sentences. Check to make sure you used correct capitalization and punctuation. Date your entry and label it with the lesson title.

Activity 3: From Sea to Shining Sea *(Offline)*
Instructions

How many hours did it take the first trains to travel from the east coast of the United States to the west coast? Complete an activity sheet to find out the answer to this and other questions.

Your work will be used to assess how well you understood the lesson.

Things really changed in 1869. What happened in Utah in that year that made it possible to move people and goods quickly over great distances? [1]

Transportation was a big part of the Industrial Revolution. Railroads brought big changes. In the United States, the railroad linked the Atlantic to the Pacific and put Americans on the move.

Complete the From Sea to Shining Sea activity sheet. Some of your work will be used to assess how well you understood the lesson.

Guided Learning: When you have finished, check your answers to questions 4-10 in the Teacher Guide.

Activity 4. Optional: Americans Climb Aboard *(Online)*
Instructions

Learn more about the transcontinental railroad. Check your library or bookstore for *Building the Transcontinental Railroad*, by Monica Halpern.

ASSESS

Lesson Assessment: Americans Climb Aboard (*Online*)

Have an adult review your answers to the Sea to Shining Sea Activity Sheet, and input the results online.

Name _____ Date _____

From Sea to Shining Sea

1. The Industrial Revolution included a revolution in _____.

2. What made it possible to move people and goods quickly over great distances?

   _____

   _____

3. How did Americans first connect their country from the Atlantic Ocean to the Pacific Ocean?

   _____

   _____

Use the U.S. Railroads, 1870 map to help you answer the following questions. Look on the next page for help in solving these problems.

4. Approximately how many miles of track were laid between Sacramento and Ogden City? Circle the answer. Then add this number to the Distances box on the map.

   224   480   625

5. In the first days of transcontinental railway travel, steam locomotives could travel 30 miles an hour. How many hours would it have taken for a train going this fast to travel from Omaha to Ogden City?

   _____

6. In the Distances box on the map, the distance from St. Louis to Chicago has been left off. Use the following information to figure out the distance, and then add this distance to the box.

   > You left St. Louis at 8 a.m. aboard a passenger train. You arrived in Chicago at 4 p.m. on the same day. The train traveled 30 miles per hour. How many miles did you travel? _____

From Sea to Shining Sea

7. If a train made the trip from New York City to Baltimore in four hours, how fast was it going?

_____

8. A team could lay five miles of track in one day. How many days would it take to lay track from Omaha to Kansas City?

_____

9. How many miles would you travel going from New York City to Sacramento by train? (Hint: Don't use the map's scale to figure this out. Use the Distances table!)

_____

10. On the roads of the 1870s, stagecoaches averaged about 70 miles per day. About how many days would it take to travel from Chicago to St. Louis by stagecoach? (Round to the nearest whole day.)

_____

Working with Distance, Time, and Speed Problems

To find distance traveled: speed × time = distance

Example: 60 miles per hour (MPH) × 5 hours = 300 miles

To find speed of travel: distance ÷ time = speed

For example: 300 miles ÷ 5 hours = 60 MPH

To find travel time: distance ÷ speed = time

For example: 300 miles ÷ 60 MPH = 5 hours

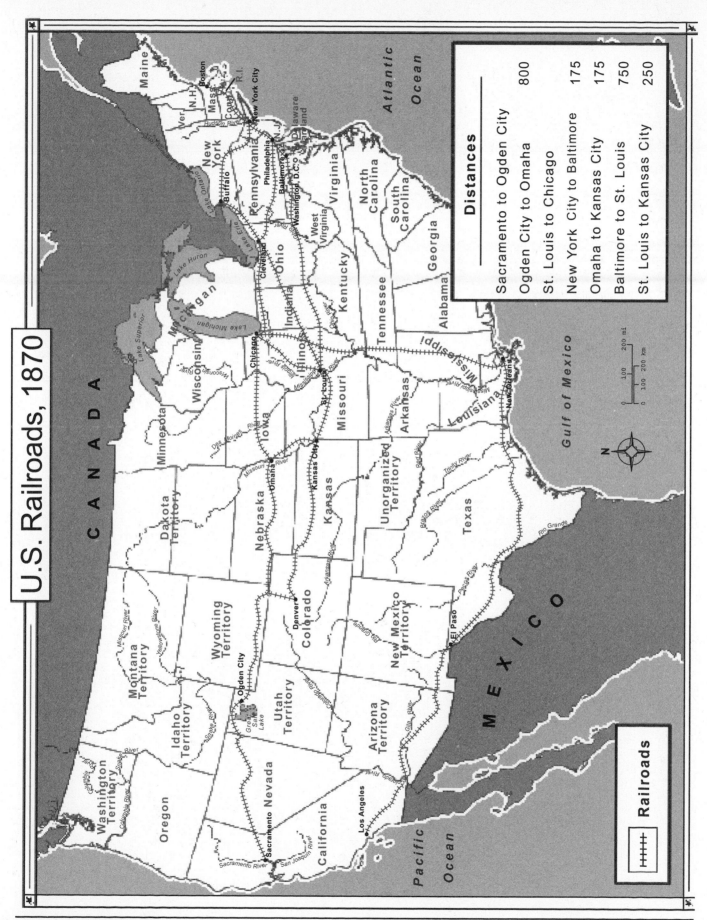

U.S. Railroads, 1870

Distances

Sacramento to Ogden City	800
Ogden City to Omaha	175
St. Louis to Chicago	175
New York City to Baltimore	175
Omaha to Kansas City	175
Baltimore to St. Louis	750
St. Louis to Kansas City	250

Railroads

Lesson Assessment

Americans Climb Aboard

1. The Industrial Revolution included a revolution in _____.

2. What made it possible to move people and goods quickly over great distances? _____

3. How did Americans first connect their country from the Atlantic Ocean to the Pacific Ocean? _____

Student Guide
Lesson 5: The First Factories

More changes came with the new power-driven looms and large machines. People no longer did most of their work at home or in artisans' shops. Instead, they worked in factories. The first factories were often dark and dangerous. They forced huge changes in the rhythm of people's lives.

Lesson Objectives

- Explain that until the Industrial Revolution, most production of goods took place in homes and cottages.
- Explain that during the Industrial Revolution, power machinery was used in factories to produce many goods.
- Recognize that the first factories were textile mills.
- List two characteristics of early factory life (long regular hours, repetitious work, poor lighting, dangerous working conditions, child labor).

PREPARE

Approximate lesson time is 60 minutes.

Materials

For the Student

Lyddie by Katherine Paterson

Keywords and Pronunciation

piecer : A mill worker who put pieces of broken thread back together.

scavenger : A mill worker who picked up bits of fallen cotton.

LEARN
Activity 1: The Hard Life of Factory Workers (Online)

Activity 2: History Journal (Offline)
Instructions

It's time to add another chapter to the story of the past. Follow the directions to complete a new entry in your History Journal.

Turn to a new page in your History Journal. On this page, write a paragraph that tells what the lesson was about.

Begin with a topic sentence that introduces the paragraph. Include at least three sentences that give details about the lesson. End with a concluding sentence. You may use the Show You Know questions to help you get started.

When you have finished, check your work. Make sure you have written in complete sentences. Check to make sure you used correct capitalization and punctuation. Date your entry and label it with the lesson title.

Guided Learning: Compare your paragraph with the one in the Lesson Guide.

Activity 3: Sarah's Neighbor Speaks to Parliament (Offline)

Instructions

You have a chance to speak before the British Parliament. What will you tell them about conditions in the first factories?

Imagine you're one of Sarah Brown's neighbors. Like her, you work in a textile factory.

Parliament is thinking about making some new laws. These laws would shorten the workday for textile workers. They would also improve working conditions. You've been asked to give a speech to the members of Parliament. You plan to talk about the terrible working conditions in the factories. You might help persuade them to pass the laws.

Write a short speech. It should describe the working conditions you face each day in the factory. Reread *Sarah's World* if you have trouble deciding what to include.

If you have time, practice your speech. Try practicing in front of a mirror--it's often helpful. Then give your speech to an audience, imaginary or real.

ASSESS

Lesson Assessment: The First Factories (*Online*)

You will complete an online assessment covering the main objectives of this lesson. Your assessment will be scored by the computer.

LEARN

Activity 4. Optional: The First Factories (Online)

Check your library or bookstore for *Lyddie*, by Katherine Paterson. In this novel, Lyddie is a Vermont farm girl. She goes to work in a textile mill in Massachusetts.

Student Guide
Lesson 6: Capitalism and New Wealth

Back in 1776, Adam Smith published a book with some very important ideas. He said that governments should let people make their own decisions about how to invest their money, or *capital*. He said that this would make nations richer. These ideas led to a system called *capitalism*. And that system made the Industrial Revolution possible.

Lesson Objectives

- Define *economy* as the way goods and services are produced and distributed.
- Name capitalism as a system in which individuals and private companies make decisions about the economy.
- Identify Adam Smith as a philosopher who wrote about capitalism.
- Name Great Britain's economy as the first capitalist economy.

PREPARE

Approximate lesson time is 60 minutes.

Materials

For the Student

📖 Let the People Decide

Keywords and Pronunciation

capitalism : A system in which individuals and companies make decisions about the economy.

economics : The study of how economies work.

economy : The way goods and services are produced and distributed.

LEARN
Activity 1: Adam Smith Has a Capital Idea *(Online)*

Activity 2: History Journal *(Offline)*

Instructions

It's time to add another chapter to the story of the past. Follow the directions to complete a new entry in your History Journal.

Turn to a new page in your History Journal. On this page, write a paragraph that tells what the lesson was about.

Begin with a topic sentence that introduces the paragraph. Include at least three sentences that give details about the lesson. End with a concluding sentence. You may use the Show You Know questions to help you get started.

When you have finished, check your work. Make sure you have written in complete sentences. Check to make sure you used correct capitalization and punctuation. Date your entry and label it with the lesson title.

Guided Learning: Compare your paragraph with the one in the Teacher Guide.

Activity 3: Let the People Decide *(Offline)*
Instructions
Adam Smith's ideas about how the economy should work caught on quickly. Ask an adult to help you complete the Let the People Decide activity sheet.

The *economy* is the way goods and services are produced and sold. In some countries, the government makes decisions about producing, buying, and selling--who can buy and sell, what they can buy and sell, and how much can be bought and sold. This is a *command* economy.

Adam Smith's ideas for how the economy should work is called *capitalism*. *Market* economy is another name for capitalism. In this type of economy, the government doesn't make those decisions about the way goods and services are produced and sold. In a capitalist, or market economy, citizens and companies make those decisions.

Complete the Let the People Decide activity sheet to see examples of how capitalism works.

Guided Learning: Check your answers with the ones in the Teacher's Guide.

ASSESS
Lesson Assessment: Capitalism and New Wealth (*Online*)
You will complete an online assessment covering the main objectives of this lesson. Your assessment will be scored by the computer.

Name _____   Date _____

Let the People Decide

Think back to James Shields, the carpenter who built a fortune as a trader. As a British citizen, he enjoyed the benefits of living in a country that had a capitalist economy.

 Activity in a market economy is made up of transactions that involve:

- Goods: things that can satisfy people's wants
- Services: actions that are valued by others
- Consumers: people who buy or rent goods or services and use them
- Producers: people who make goods or provide services

In the story about James Shields:

1. What goods did James Shields supply?

   _____

2. What service was Shields providing?

   _____

3. Who were the consumers for the sugar Shields was shipping?

   _____

   Who were the consumers for the clothes and tools he was shipping?

   _____

4. Name two producers in this story.

   _____

Supply is the goods and services that sellers are willing and able to sell. *Demand* is the goods and services that buyers are willing and able to purchase. *Supply* and *demand* is an important part of a capitalist economy.

5. Why was there a demand for sugar in England? Why is there a demand for sugar today?

_____

_____

6. Why do you think there was a demand for English clothes and tools in the West Indies?

_____

_____

7. Do you think Shields would have been successful if he had tried to supply sugar to the West Indies? Why or why not?

_____

_____

Cost is the money is takes to make and sell goods and services.

Revenue is money that is received in return for selling goods and services.

Profit is total revenue minus total costs.

Loss is the amount of money lost when total revenue is less than total costs.

Let's use an example of a company in Boston that makes furniture.

Cost

The company's costs would include things such as:

- The cost of lumber from a sawmill
- The cost of renting the building where the furniture is made
- The cost of paying skilled workers to make the furniture
- The cost of printing advertising handbills to advertise the furniture

For this example, let's say it costs the company $5.00 to make and sell one table.

Revenue

The company's revenue is the money it receives when it sells the furniture to its customers. If a table sells for $10.00 and the company sells 10 tables in one month, its revenue for that month is $100.00.

Profit

Let's say the company makes 20 tables in the month of October and sells all of them by the end of the month. The company's profit for that month would be $100.00.

Revenue	minus	Costs	=	Profit
20 × $10.00 = $200.00	–	20 × $5.00 = $100.00	=	profit
$200.00	–	$100.00	=	$100.00

8. What would the company's profits be if it had produced 20 tables and sold only 18 of them?

_____

Loss

Losses aren't good. They mean that a company is losing money. Let's imagine that the furniture company made 30 tables in November. It was able to sell only 10 of them. The company would have losses of $50.00 for that month. This is because the total revenue was $100.00, but the total costs were $150.00. Total revenue was less than the total costs.

9. If the company made 50 tables one month and sold 23, would they have made a profit or suffered losses?

_____

What would the profit or loss be?

_____

Student Guide
Lesson 7. Optional: Charles Dickens: From Boy to Author

Charles Dickens was one of the greatest writers in the English language. As a boy, he was well educated, but his family fell into money troubles. His father went to debtors' prison, and young Charles had to go to work in a factory. He experienced the life of the poor. Later he would write about it.

Lesson Objectives

- Identify Charles Dickens as a great author of the nineteenth century.
- Explain that as a boy Charles Dickens worked in a factory and experienced the life of the poor.
- Name two of Charles Dickens's famous works.

PREPARE

Approximate lesson time is 60 minutes.

Materials

> For the Student
>> History Journal
>> 🖥 Counting Centuries

Keywords and Pronunciation

debtors' prison : A prison for people who could not pay their debts.

LEARN
Activity 1. Optional: Optional Lesson Instructions *(Online)*

Activity 2. Optional: A Dickens of a Time *(Online)*

Activity 3. Optional: History Journal *(Offline)*
Instructions

It's time to add another chapter to the story of the past. Follow the directions in the Student Guide to complete a new entry in your History Journal.

Turn to a new page in your History Journal. On this page, write a paragraph that tells what the lesson was about. Your work will be used to assess how well you understood the lesson.

Begin with a topic sentence that introduces the paragraph. Include at least three sentences that give details about the lesson. End with a concluding sentence. You may use the Show You Know questions to help you get started.

Your paragraph should include answers to the following questions:

1. Who was Charles Dickens?
2. How did Dickens know about the lives of poor factory workers?
3. What country, in what period of history, did most of Dickens's stories deal with?

When you have finished, check your work. Make sure you have written in complete sentences. Then check to make sure you used correct capitalization and punctuation. Date your entry and label it with the lesson title.

Guided Learning: Compare your paragraph with the one in the Teacher Guide.

Activity 4. Optional: Counting Centuries (Offline)

Instructions

Complete the Counting Centuries activity sheet, which will help you to understand what centuries are.

Do you remember when the Declaration of Independence was signed? July 4, 1776. It was signed in the eighteenth century. That might seem a little odd--it was signed in the 1700s, but in the *eighteenth* century. It seems as if it should be the *seventeenth* century, doesn't it?

Print and complete the Counting Centuries activity sheet. After you've finished, this might not seem odd anymore.

Guided Learning: Have an adult check your answers.

Activity 5. Optional: Charles Dickens: From Boy to Author (Offline)

Many of Dickens's stories have been made into movies. Two of these are listed in the Student Guide.

Charles Dickens's stories and characters are loved all over the world. Many of his novels have been made into movies. *A Christmas Carol* and *Oliver Twist* are two of his works that have been adapted for the big screen. These two movies are musicals.

- *Scrooge* (based on *A Christmas Carol*), 1970, Twentieth Century Fox (86 minutes, rated G)
- *Oliver!* (based on *Oliver Twist*), 1968, Columbia/Tristar Pictures (145 minutes, rated G)

Name _____ Date _____

Counting Centuries

A century is a period of time that covers one hundred years. The time from 1900 to 1999 was a period of one hundred years. So was the time from 1800 to 1899. Centuries are a convenient way to divide up a really long span of time.

But when you're dealing with centuries, there's something to keep in mind. The number of a century is always a hundred years later than the numbers of the years in that century. For example, the nineteenth century refers to the period of time between 1800 and 1899. The twentieth century refers to the period of time between 1900 and 1999. With a little practice you can always figure out which century any year is in.

Use this formula to help you figure out the century: Year plus a hundred equals century. For example, if you wanted to know in what century the Declaration of Independence was signed, take the year, 1776, and add a hundred.

$$
\begin{array}{r}
1776 \\
+\ 100 \\
\hline
\mathbf{1876}
\end{array}
$$

Just look at the first two digits—that's the century. The Declaration of Independence was signed in the eighteenth century.

You can use this mnemonic to help you remember the formula: **Y**ellow **p**ancakes **h**elp **e**lephants **c**ry (**y**ear **p**lus a **h**undred **e**quals **c**entury).

Now let's practice!

Counting Centuries

1. James Watt developed his steam engine during the 1770s. So the first practical steam engine was invented in the _____ century.

2. The Scientific Revolution began around 1600. In what century did it begin? _____

3. Charles Dickens was born in 1812 and died in 1870. He lived during the _____ century.

4. Napoleon was defeated at Waterloo in the beginning of the nineteenth century. The exact date was June 18, _____15. (Fill in the first two numbers of the year.)

5. If something happened in the 1900s, in what century did it happen? _____

Finally, here's a riddle for you: "I am a product. I have two factors. One of my factors is the last year of the fifteenth century. My other factor is half of a pair. What am I?"

_____

Answer to riddle: 1499. Explanation: The last year of the fifteenth century is 1499. Half of a pair is 1.

(A pair is 2; half of 2 is 1.) 1499 × 1 = 1499

Student Guide
Lesson 8. Optional: Charles Dickens, the Author

Charles Dickens wrote books that captured hearts. He held a mirror up to England. He wrote things that made people laugh. But he also wrote about the hard life of the poor in England during the Industrial Revolution.

Lesson Objectives

- Describe working and living conditions for the urban poor in Dickens's time.
- Explain that Charles Dickens used his writing to move people to try to solve the problems of the cities and make life better for the workers.

PREPARE

Approximate lesson time is 60 minutes.

Materials

    For the Student

        History Journal

        🖳 From A Christmas Carol by Charles Dickens

LEARN
Activity 1. Optional: Optional Lesson Instructions *(Online)*

Activity 2. Optional: The Very Dickens *(Online)*

Activity 3. Optional: History Journal *(Offline)*
Instructions

It's time to add another chapter to the story of the past. Follow the directions to complete a new entry in your History Journal.

Turn to a new page in your History Journal. On this page, write a paragraph that tells what the lesson was about. Be sure to identify at least two of Dickens's famous works.

Begin with a topic sentence that introduces the paragraph. Include at least three sentences that give details about the lesson. End with a concluding sentence. You may use the Show You Know questions to help you get started.

When you have finished, check your work. Make sure you have written in complete sentences. Check to make sure you used correct capitalization and punctuation. Date your entry and label it with the lesson title.

Guided Learning: Compare your paragraph with the one in the Teacher Guide.

Activity 4. Optional: Charles Dickens, the Author *(Offline)*
Instructions

Find a passage from one of Dickens's novels that interests you. Practice giving a dramatic reading of the passage. Then invite family and friends to listen.

You can pick your own passage from Dickens's writing, or print the selection from *A Christmas Carol*.

Name _____   Date _____

From *A Christmas Carol*, by Charles Dickens

Oh! But he was a tight-fisted hand at the grind-stone, Scrooge! a squeezing, wrenching, grasping, scraping, clutching, covetous, old sinner! Hard and sharp as flint, from which no steel had ever struck out generous fire; secret, and self-contained, and solitary as an oyster. The cold within him froze his old features, nipped his pointed nose, shriveled his cheek, stiffened his gait; made his eyes red, his thin lips blue; and spoke out shrewdly in his grating voice….

Once upon a time—of all the good days in the year, on Christmas Eve— old Scrooge sat busy in his counting-house. It was cold, bleak, biting weather, foggy withal, and he could hear the people in the court outside, go wheezing up and down, beating their hands upon their breasts, and stamping their feet upon the pavement stones to warm them….

"A merry Christmas, uncle! God save you!" cried a cheerful voice. It was the voice of Scrooge's nephew.

"Bah!" said Scrooge, "Humbug!"

He had so heated himself with rapid walking in the fog and frost, this nephew of Scrooge's, that he was all in a glow; his face was ruddy and handsome; his eyes sparkled, and his breath smoked again.

"Christmas a humbug, uncle!" said Scrooge's nephew. "You don't mean that, I am sure?"

"I do," said Scrooge. "Merry Christmas! What right have you to be merry? What reason have you to be merry? You're poor enough."

"Come, then," returned the nephew gaily. "What right have you to be dismal? What reason have you to be morose? You're rich enough."

Scrooge having no better answer ready on the spur of the moment, said, "Bah!" again; and followed it up with "Humbug."

"Don't be cross, uncle!" said the nephew.

"What else can I be," returned the uncle, "when I live in such a world of fools as this? Merry Christmas! Out upon merry Christmas! What's Christmas time to you but a time for paying bills without money; a time for finding yourself a year older, but not an hour richer? If I could work my will," said Scrooge indignantly, "every idiot who goes about with 'Merry Christmas' on his lips, should be boiled with his own pudding, and buried with a stake of holly through his heart. He should!"

From *A Christmas Carol*, by Charles Dickens

"Uncle!" pleaded the nephew.

"Nephew!" returned the uncle sternly, "keep Christmas in your own way, and let me keep it in mine."

"Keep it!" repeated Scrooge's nephew. "But you don't keep it."

"Let me leave it alone, then," said Scrooge. "Much good may it do you! Much good it has ever done you!"

"There are many things from which I might have derived good, by which I have not profited, I dare say," returned the nephew. "But I am sure I have always thought of Christmas time … as a good time; a kind, forgiving, charitable, pleasant time…. And therefore, uncle, though it has never put a scrap of gold or silver in my pocket, I believe that it has done me good, and will do me good; and I say, God bless it!"

Student Guide
Lesson 9: Karl Marx in London

Would workers always accept their sad situation? Karl Marx said no. He said there would be a revolution. The workers would revolt against the new owners of industry. Marx's ideas, called Marxism, would be important in later years.

Lesson Objectives

- Explain that during the Industrial Revolution there were large differences in the way the rich and poor lived.
- Describe Karl Marx as a philosopher and revolutionary.
- Explain that Marx predicted a revolution in which the working classes would rise up and overthrow the owners of industry.
- Recognize that the terms *Marxism* and *communism* refer to the work and theories of Karl Marx.

PREPARE

Approximate lesson time is 60 minutes.

LEARN
Activity 1: Karl Marx and Communism *(Online)*

Activity 2: History Journal *(Offline)*
Instructions
It's time to add another chapter to the story of the past. Follow the directions to complete a new entry in your History Journal.

Turn to a new page in your History Journal. On this page, write a paragraph that tells what the lesson was about.

Begin with a topic sentence that introduces the paragraph. Include at least three sentences that give details about the lesson. End with a concluding sentence. You may use the Show You Know questions to help you get started.

When you have finished, check your work. Make sure you have written in complete sentences. Check to make sure you used correct capitalization and punctuation. Date your entry and label it with the lesson title.

Guided Learning: Compare your paragraph with the one in the Lesson Guide.

Activity 3: An Interview with Karl Marx *(Offline)*

Instructions

Imagine that the year is 1865 and you're a journalist for a London magazine. You've been given an assignment to interview Karl Marx.

Imagine you're a journalist for a London magazine. You've been given an assignment to interview Karl Marx. The interview will appear as a feature in the magazine.

Write at least four questions to ask Marx during your interview with him. For each question, write the answer you think Marx would give.

Use this format:

student: Question

Marx: His answer

student: Your next question

Marx: His answer

Before you start writing, answer these questions. The answers may help you think of your own questions to ask.

1. During the Industrial Revolution, did the rich and poor live similar lives?

2. How would you describe Karl Marx?

3. What did Karl Marx predict would happen?

4. What two words refer to the work and theories of Karl Marx?

To help you get started, here's the second question and its answer.

How would you describe Karl Marx?

Karl Marx was a philosopher and a revolutionary.

Now here's an example of a question and answer you could include in your interview.

Mike: Mr. Marx, how would you describe yourself?

Marx: I am a philosopher and a revolutionary. I think there should be big changes in the world.

ASSESS

Lesson Assessment: Karl Marx in London (*Online*)

You will complete an online assessment covering the main objectives of this lesson. Your assessment will be scored by the computer.

Student Guide
Lesson 10: The Great Exhibition

In 1851, people flocked to a giant fair in London. Great Britain led the Industrial Revolution. It had become "the workshop of the world." The Great Exhibition displayed British abilities to the world.

Lesson Objectives
- Explain that Britain had become the world's leader in the Industrial Revolution.
- Name Victoria as the British queen who reigned during this period.
- Describe the Great Exhibition as a fair that displayed British goods, abilities, and successes.
- Recognize that Britain was known as "the workshop of the world" and that the British had a strong sense of pride in their nation.

PREPARE

Approximate lesson time is 60 minutes.

Keywords and Pronunciation
Koh-i-noor (KOH-uh-noor)

LEARN
Activity 1: England and Miracles of Modern Industry *(Online)*

Activity 2: Come to the Great Exhibition! *(Offline)*
Instructions
Create a poster to advertise the Great Exhibition. Your work will be used to assess how well you understand this lesson.

More than six million people visited the Great Exhibition. People traveled there from all over the world. They all wanted to see the wonders inside the Crystal Palace. How do you think they found out about it?

Articles showed up in newspapers. Posters appeared on street corners. And news of the giant fair spread by word of mouth.

Make a poster that advertises the Great Exhibition and invites people to come and see it.

In your poster, find ways to show all these ideas:
- Britain was the leader of the Industrial Revolution.
- Victoria was the queen of England.
- The Great Exhibition displayed Britain's wealth and abilities.
- Britain was called "the workshop of the world."
- The British were proud of their country.

Be a good advertiser. Make your poster colorful and eye-catching!

174

ASSESS

Lesson Assessment: The Great Exhibition (*Online*)

Have an adult review your answers to the Come to the Great Exhibition! activity and input the results online.

LEARN

Activity 3. Optional: The Great Exhibition (*Online*)

Name _____ Date _____

Lesson Assessment

The Great Exhibition

More than six million people visited the Great Exhibition. People traveled there from all over the world. They all wanted to see the wonders inside the Crystal Palace. How do you think they found out about it?

Articles showed up in newspapers. Posters appeared on street corners. And news of the giant fair spread by word of mouth.

Make a poster that advertises the Great Exhibition and invites people to come and see it.

In your poster, find ways to show all these ideas:

- Britain was the leader of the Industrial Revolution.
- Victoria was the queen of England.
- The Great Exhibition displayed Britain's wealth and abilities.
- Britain was called "the workshop of the world."
- The British were proud of their country.

Be a good advertiser. Make your poster colorful and eye-catching!

Student Guide
Lesson 11: Unit Review and Assessment

You've completed this unit, and now it's time to review what you've learned and take the unit assessment.

Lesson Objectives

- Demonstrate mastery of important knowledge and skills in this unit.
- Recognize that many of the first innovations of the Industrial Revolution were in the textile industry.
- Identify James Hargreaves as the inventor of the spinning jenny.
- List the steamboat and better roads as major improvements in transportation.
- Identify Robert Fulton as the inventor of the first practical steamboat.
- Explain that the steam-powered locomotive made it possible to move people and goods quickly over great distances.
- Explain that Americans used the railroad to connect the country from the Atlantic to the Pacific Ocean.
- Explain that until the Industrial Revolution, most production of goods took place in homes and cottages.
- Explain that during the Industrial Revolution, power machinery was used in factories to produce many goods.
- List two characteristics of early factory life (long regular hours, repetitious work, poor lighting, dangerous working conditions, child labor).
- Name capitalism as a system in which individuals and private companies make decisions about the economy.
- Describe Karl Marx as a philosopher and revolutionary.
- Explain that Britain had become the world's leader in the Industrial Revolution.
- Name Victoria as the British queen who reigned during this period.
- Name Great Britain's economy as the first capitalist economy.
- Explain that before the Industrial Revolution, people relied on animals, water, and their own muscles for power.
- Describe steam engines as important in the Industrial Revolution because they supplied much more power.
- Identify James Watt as a Scottish engineer who designed an efficient steam engine.
- Describe the Industrial Revolution as a time when more and more goods were produced by power-driven machinery.
- Explain that the Industrial Revolution began in England.
- Explain that during the Industrial Revolution production moved out of the home and into factories.
- Explain that in the early stages of the Industrial Revolution working conditions were harsh and workers suffered.

PREPARE

Approximate lesson time is 60 minutes.

LEARN
Activity 1: The Industrial Revolution *(Offline)*

Instructions

We've covered a lot, and now it's time to take a look back. Here's what you should remember about the Industrial Revolution.

Our story of the Industrial Revolution began in a weaver's cottage. Less than one hundred years later, it filled a Crystal Palace. In what country did the Industrial Revolution start? [1]

Of course, the Industrial Revolution did more than fill the Crystal Palace at the Great Exhibition in London. It spread across the Atlantic Ocean to America. It spread across the English Channel to mainland Europe. Between 1750 and 1850, the Industrial Revolution changed the world.

What was the Industrial Revolution? It was a time when new machines and steam power made it possible to produce more than ever before. More thread. More cloth. More coal. More iron. More tools. More everything!

The British seemed to come up with one good idea after the next. They quickly took the lead in producing many goods. Do you remember the name of the weaver who figured out a new way to spin thread quickly? [2]

James Hargreaves's invention spun many threads together at once and sped up the textile industry. What was his invention called? (Hint: It was named after his daughter.) [3]

The spinning jenny helped the textile industry, but a Scottish inventor helped even more. His name was James Watt. What did James Watt invent? [4]

Watt's steam engine helped miners pump water out of mines. But people also started using the steam engine to power looms. That was another boost for the British textile industry.

But these looms powered by steam were large. Pretty soon merchants realized that these new machines and power looms could weave cloth faster if everything was together in one place. Until that time, where had most cloth been made? [5]

Before long, merchants began to put workers, spinning machines, and steam-powered looms together in big buildings called factories. By bringing them all together, the factories could produce more cloth. Factories sprang up in cities. People flocked to them from the farms.

That switch from cottage to factory and from farm to city was huge. Men, women, and children who used to work long days on their farms now started working long days in factories. The factories were often dark and dirty. The clatter of the looms was deafening. The tasks were repetitive. The supervisors were strict. Nobody enjoyed working in a factory. Still, many people were glad to find a job there and earn money for their families. British factories pumped out more goods than ever before.

But it would not be very helpful to produce a lot of goods if it was hard to get those goods to market. A revolution in transportation was about to become part of the Industrial Revolution.

An inventive American started to think hard about using the steam engine to power a boat. Who invented the first practical steamboat? [6]

Steamboats in the United States and in England raced new goods inland. But what about roads? If inland roads were only bumpy cow paths, it would be hard to move things to market. Along came John McAdam. What did he invent? [7]

McAdam's road paving was so successful that today we still talk about paving with "macadam."

Steamboats and good roads were only the beginning. The steam-powered locomotive moved people and things a lot further. Which country soon took the lead in building railroads? [8]

Why were people there so interested in railroads? [9]

Miles of iron rail soon made it possible to travel from one place to the next at nearly a mile a minute!

Meanwhile, back in England, the city of London became a hub of the new industrial life. Factories sprang up in the south end. Poor neighborhoods surrounded them. Rich shop and factory owners lived in nice neighborhoods in London's east end.

London was abuzz with life. More shops and markets were everywhere. More wealth was everywhere. What was the name of the economic system the English used to make all this to happen? [10]

Capitalism meant that individuals and private companies owned the means of production. People who owned textile factories and shops became wealthy.

What great English writer observed and wrote about life in London in the nineteenth century? [11]

Charles Dickens made many people think hard about the high price of the new Industrial Revolution. He wrote about abandoned street children, struggling families, and wealthy shop owners. How did Dickens know so much about all this? [12]

Another writer was thinking about these issues, too. He was a German philosopher living in London. He was a critic of capitalism. What was his name? [13]

Karl Marx said capitalism was very good at producing wealth. But he said capitalism was not very good at spreading that wealth among many people. Why should the owners of factories have everything and workers so little? Karl Marx said workers wouldn't put up with this for long. There would be a revolution of workers against the owners of industry. Can you guess what Marx's ideas are called? [14]

In the 1850s, while Charles Dickens and Karl Marx were writing, the British wanted to show the world how far they'd come. Who was queen of England at the time? [15]

During the reign of Victoria, the British organized their Great Exhibition at the Crystal Palace in London. Do you remember what the Great Exhibition displayed? [16]

Kings, queens, dukes and emperors visited the display. They were astonished. Great Britain became known as the workshop of the world. It led the way in an Industrial Revolution that would change the entire world.

Activity 2: History Journal Review (Offline)

Instructions

It's time to prepare for the unit assessment by reviewing your History Journal.

Use your History Journal to review the unit called The Industrial Revolution. Take some time to go over the work you've done. An adult can also help you review by asking you questions based on the work in your journal.

Activity 3: Online Interactive Review (Online)

ASSESS

Unit Assessment: The Industrial Revolution (Offline)

Complete an offline Unit Assessment. Your learning coach will score this part of the Assessment.

Name _____   Date _____

The Industrial Revolution

Read each question and its answer choices. Fill in the bubble in front of the word or words that best answer each question.

1. Many of the first innovations of the Industrial Revolution made England a leader in what industry?

   ⓐ wine production

   ⓑ shipbuilding

   ⓒ textile manufacture

   ⓓ hotels

2. Why were steam engines important in the Industrial Revolution?

   ⓐ They provided a lot more power than people and animals could.

   ⓑ They supplied electricity to homes and factories.

   ⓒ They made it possible to build skyscrapers.

   ⓓ They moved production from the factory to the home.

3. What was one big effect of the Industrial Revolution?

   ⓐ More and more goods were produced by powerful machines.

   ⓑ More nations abandoned factories and steam engines.

   ⓒ Farmland became available to English shepherds and peasants.

   ⓓ A revolution of workers took place in England.

4. What made it possible to move people and goods quickly over great distances in the 1800s?

    ⓐ   stagecoaches

    ⓑ   steam-powered locomotives

    ⓒ   prairie schooners

    ⓓ   airplanes

5. Before the Industrial Revolution, where did most production of goods take place?

    ⓐ   in factories

    ⓑ   in homes and cottages

    ⓒ   in schools and monasteries

    ⓓ   in office buildings

6. In what economic system are individual people and private companies in charge of making economic choices?

    ⓐ   communism

    ⓑ   socialism

    ⓒ   capitalism

    ⓓ   traditionalism

7. Which country had the world's first capitalist economy?

    ⓐ   France

    ⓑ   Great Britain

    ⓒ   Germany

    ⓓ   Portugal

8. During the Industrial Revolution, Britain was known as "the workshop of the world." Why?

    (a)   Britain was the leader of the Industrial Revolution.

    (b)   Most of the world's workers lived there.

    (c)   Britain produced more railroad track than any other country.

    (d)   All of the world's crystal was made there.

9. What philosopher living in London wrote about class struggle and against owners of industry?

    (a)   James Hargreaves

    (b)   Charles Dickens

    (c)   Karl Marx

    (d)   Prince Albert

10. What country took the lead in building railroads?

    (a)   Germany

    (b)   Ireland

    (c)   the United States

    (d)   France

11. During the early Industrial Revolution, what were working conditions like for factory workers?

    (a)   The factories were well lit and clean, but the hours were long.

    (b)   The hours were long and the factories were dark and unsafe.

    (c)   Women and children worked few hours, but men worked long hours.

    (d)   The pay was good, and most people were quite happy.

12. Which of these were major improvements in transportation during the Industrial Revolution?

ⓐ highways and monorails

ⓑ submarines and airplanes

ⓒ sailing ships and hot air balloons

ⓓ steamboats and better roads

Match the name of each person on the left with a description of the person on the right. Write the letter of the description on the line in front of the name. There is one extra description on the right that does not match any of the names.

13. _____ James Hargreaves

_____ James Watt

_____ Robert Fulton

_____ Victoria

A. Inventor of the first practical steamboat

B. Queen of England during the Industrial Revolution

C. Improved the paving of roads

D. Inventor of the spinning jenny

E Designed an efficient steam engine

14. Write a paragraph about the Industrial Revolution. Include the following.

- Tell where the Industrial Revolution started.
- Explain how the production of goods changed.
- Explain what effect this had on where people lived.
- Describe what factory life was like.

A topic sentence is provided. Write neatly in complete sentences. Check your spelling, capitalization, and punctuation. End your paragraph with a concluding sentence.

Between 1750 and 1850, the Industrial Revolution changed the world. _____

_____

_____

_____

_____

_____

_____

_____

_____

_____

_____

_____

Student Guide
Lesson 1: A New Kind of Czar: Peter the Great

In Europe, old kingdoms disappeared and new nations burst onto the scene. The countries of Germany, Italy, and Greece took their places on the map. Russian czars tried to drag their empire into modern times. Meanwhile, across the Atlantic, Americans were building their democratic nation. The United States suffered its greatest test as a union--and survived.

Peter the Great was very interested in the changes that were happening in western Europe. He tried to bring western ways to Russia. Sometimes the Russian people did not want change. But Peter the Great insisted.

Lesson Objectives

- Explain that many nations came into being and grew stronger at this time.
- Describe nationalism as a strong sense of pride in one's nation.
- Describe the growth of Russia, and name some major Russian leaders (Peter the Great, Catherine the Great, Nicholas II).
- Name Germany and Italy as two European nations that developed into single countries in the nineteenth century.
- State that the question of whether to allow slavery's expansion into the new American territories led to a bloody civil war won by the North.
- Identify key figures and events that promoted nationalism (Ypsilanti, Lincoln, U.S. Civil War, Brothers Grimm, Bismarck, Garibaldi).
- Explain that the first modern Olympics began in the late 1800s with the growth of nationalism.
- Locate Russia and the Ural Mountains on a map.
- Define *czar* as the Russian leader.
- Describe Peter the Great as a czar who tried to bring western ways to Russia.
- Name St. Petersburg as the city built by Peter the Great.

PREPARE

Approximate lesson time is 60 minutes.

Materials

For the Student

    🖥 Map of Europe, 1725

    🖥 Map of Russia, 1725-1855

Keywords and Pronunciation

czar (zahr) : The Russian ruler.

nationalism : a strong feeling of attachment to one´s own country

Okhotsk (uh-KAWTSK)

Urals (YOUR-uhls)

LEARN

Activity 1: A Great Country and Its Great Czar *(Online)*

Peter the Great was a big man with big plans for Russia. He learned about the Scientific Revolution and the Industrial Revolution. He worked hard to bring modern ideas from western Europe to his old-fashioned country. Learn how this big man worked at his big dreams.

Activity 2: History Journal *(Offline)*

Instructions

It's time to add another chapter to the story of the past. Follow the directions to complete a new entry in your History Journal.

Turn to a new page in your History Journal. On this page, write a paragraph that tells what the lesson was about. Your work will be used to assess how well you understood the lesson.

Begin with a topic sentence that introduces the paragraph. Include at least three sentences that give details about the lesson. End with a concluding sentence. You may use the Show You Know questions to help you get started.

When you have finished, check your work. Make sure you have written in complete sentences. Check to make sure you used correct capitalization and punctuation. Date your entry and label it with the lesson title.

Guided Learning: Compare your paragraph with the one in the Teacher Guide. Then point to Russia and the Ural Mountains on your map.

Activity 3: Peter the Great in Europe *(Online)*

Activity 4. Optional: A New Kind of Czar: Peter the Great *(Online)*

ASSESS

Lesson Assessment: A New Kind of Czar: Peter the Great (*Online*)

Have an adult review your answers to the History Journal activity, and input the results online.

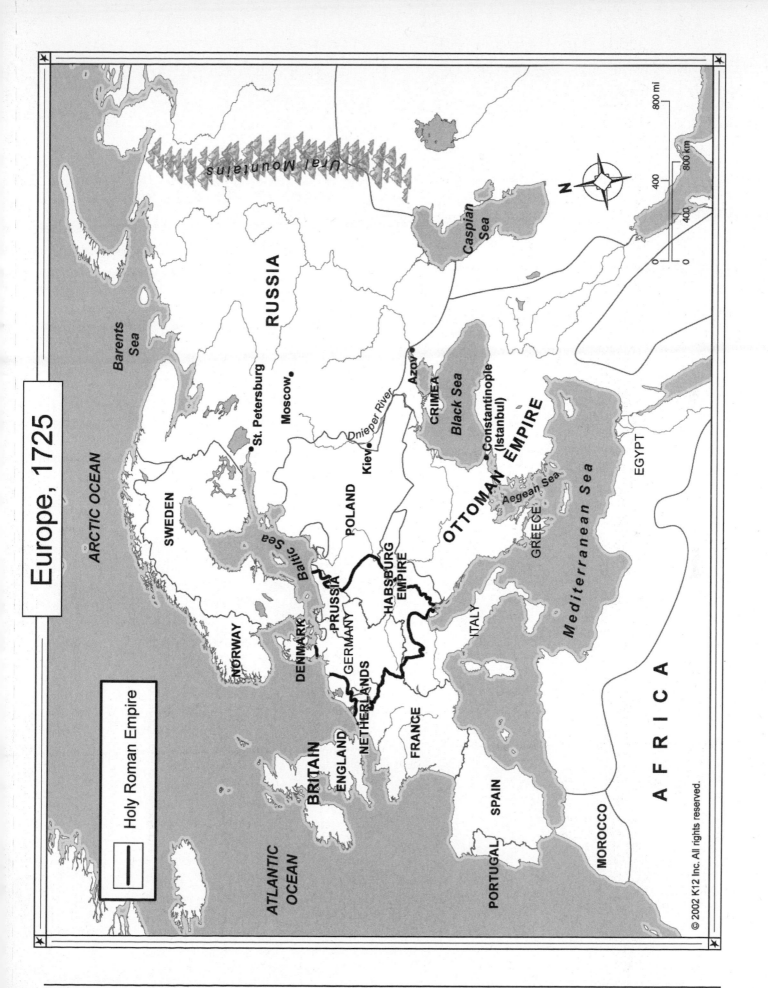

Europe, 1725

Holy Roman Empire

ARCTIC OCEAN

Barents
Sea

Ural Mountains

RUSSIA

St. Petersburg
Moscow

Caspian
Sea

Azov
CRIMEA
Black Sea
Constantinople
(Istanbul)

Dnieper River
Kiev

POLAND

OTTOMAN EMPIRE

SWEDEN

Baltic Sea

NORWAY

DENMARK

PRUSSIA

GERMANY

NETHERLANDS

HABSBURG
EMPIRE

Aegean Sea

GREECE

ITALY

EGYPT

Mediterranean Sea

BRITAIN

ENGLAND

FRANCE

ATLANTIC
OCEAN

SPAIN

PORTUGAL

MOROCCO

A F R I C A

N

800 mi
400
0

800 km
400
0

© 2002 K12 Inc. All rights reserved.

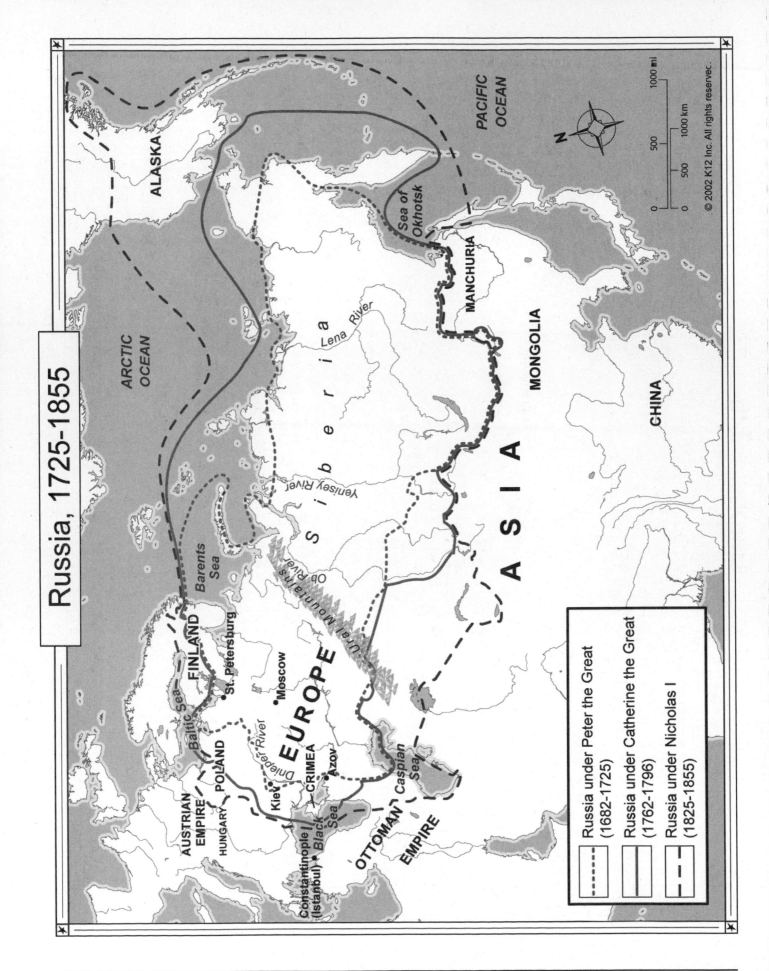

Russia, 1725-1855

ALASKA

PACIFIC OCEAN

ARCTIC OCEAN

Barents Sea

Sea of Okhotsk

S i b e r i a

Lena River

Yenisey River

Ob River

Ural Mountains

MANCHURIA

MONGOLIA

A S I A

CHINA

EUROPE

FINLAND

Baltic Sea

St. Petersburg

•Moscow

Dnieper River

POLAND

AUSTRIAN EMPIRE

HUNGARY

Kiev•

CRIMEA

Azov

Black Sea

Constantinople (Istanbul)•

OTTOMAN EMPIRE

Caspian Sea

Legend:
- Russia under Peter the Great (1682-1725)
- Russia under Catherine the Great (1762-1796)
- Russia under Nicholas I (1825-1855)

1000 mi
1000 km
500
500
0
0

N

Name _____   Date _____

Lesson Assessment

A New Kind of Czar: Peter the Great

1. Use the *Map of Russia, 1725-1855* to locate the Ural Mountains.

2. Turn to a new page in your History Journal. On this page, write a paragraph that tells what the lesson was about. Your work will be used to assess how well you understood the lesson.

    Begin with a topic sentence that introduces the paragraph. Include at least three sentences that give details about the lesson. End with a concluding sentence. You may use the Show You Know questions to help you get started.

    When you have finished, check your work. Make sure you have written in complete sentences. Check to make sure you used correct capitalization and punctuation.

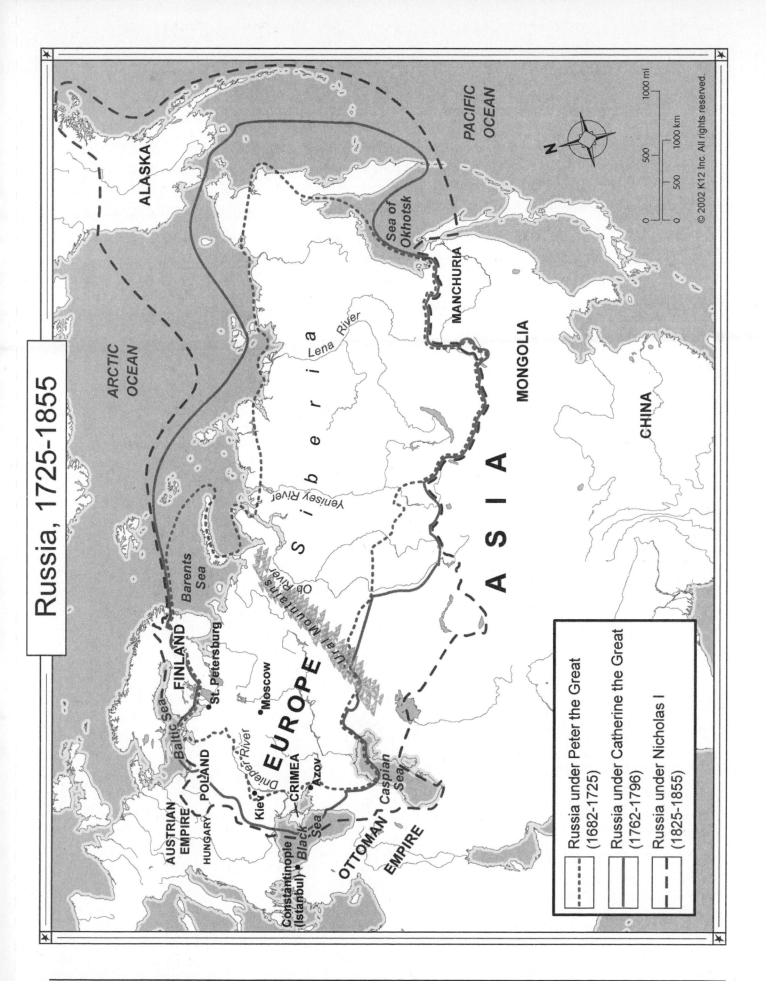

Russia, 1725-1855

ALASKA

PACIFIC OCEAN

ARCTIC OCEAN

Barents Sea

Sea of Okhotsk

Lena River

S i b e r i a

Yenisey River

Ob River

Ural Mountains

MANCHURIA

MONGOLIA

CHINA

A S I A

E U R O P E

FINLAND

St. Petersburg

• Moscow

Dnieper River

POLAND

AUSTRIAN EMPIRE

HUNGARY

Kiev •

CRIMEA

• Azov

Black Sea

Constantinople (Istanbul) •

OTTOMAN EMPIRE

Caspian Sea

Baltic Sea

1000 mi

1000 km

500

500

© 2002 K12 Inc. All rights reserved.

	Russia under Peter the Great (1682-1725)
	Russia under Catherine the Great (1762-1796)
	Russia under Nicholas I (1825-1855)

Student Guide
Lesson 2: Catherine the Great

Catherine the Great ruled Russia for more than 30 years. Like Peter the Great, this empress was attracted to western ideas. She expanded Russia's borders. But the lives of serfs in Russia remained hard during her reign.

Lesson Objectives

- Explain that serfdom grew under Catherine the Great's reign.
- Explain that Catherine the Great expanded Russia to the Black Sea.
- Describe Catherine as attracted to western ideas.
- Identify Catherine the Great as an empress of Russia.

PREPARE

Approximate lesson time is 60 minutes.

Materials

For the Student

- 🖳 Map of Russia, 1725-1855
- 🖳 Sea Routes to Southern Russia activity sheet
- 🖳 Build a Potemkin Village Worksheet

Keywords and Pronunciation

ambassador : An official who goes to another country to represent his or her own country.

Crimea (kriy-MEE-uh)

czar (zahr) : The Russian ruler.

Dnieper (NEE-pur)

Grigory Potemkin (grih-GOR-ee poh-TEM-kin)

Kiev (KEE-ef)

LEARN
Activity 1: Russia Gets Another "Great" Leader *(Online)*

Activity 2: History Journal *(Offline)*
Instructions

It's time to add another chapter to the story of the past. Follow the directions to complete a new entry in your History Journal.

Turn to a new page in your History Journal. On this page, write a paragraph that tells what the lesson was about.

Begin with a topic sentence that introduces the paragraph. Include at least three sentences that give details about the lesson. End with a concluding sentence. You may use the Show You Know questions to help you get started.

When you have finished, check your work. Make sure you have written in complete sentences. Check to make sure you used correct capitalization and punctuation. Date your entry and label it with the lesson title.

Guided Learning: Compare your paragraph with the one in the Teacher Guide.

Activity 3: The Crimea: Russia's Southern Trading Door *(Offline)*
Instructions

The Crimea is Russia's southern door to shipping. Map out the best trade routes to and from the Crimea so that Russian merchants can make Russia rich!

Catherine the Great expanded Russia in several directions. She was especially interested in the area of the Black Sea. That was because Russia had always had a problem getting ships in and out of its ports.

Look at the map of Russia. Its entire northern boundary borders the sea. So does its eastern boundary. But the Arctic Ocean to the north is frozen in the winter. That means that ships can't get in or out. And the Pacific Ocean to the east is far away. Remember that most Russians lived west of the Ural Mountains. It was difficult and expensive to get goods from eastern Russia to western Russia.

Russians wanted seaports that were open year-round. And they wanted their ports to be closer to the trade routes of Asia, Africa, Europe, and the Americas. The Crimean Peninsula on the northern edge of the Black Sea offered that. In 1783, under Catherine the Great, Crimea became a part of Russia.

Imagine that you are a Russian merchant who owns several trading ships. You want to trade with the rest of the world to make yourself and Russia rich. On the Sea Routes to Southern Russia activity sheet, draw trade routes that your ships could follow to trade with these places: Turkey, Egypt, Italy, France, Spain, Morocco, England, and the Americas.

Trade routes are only good if ships can get by. If somebody wanted to stop your ships from getting by, what two points on the map are best for the control of the shipping trade? Why?

Guided Learning: Compare your routes and answers with those in the Teacher Guide.

Activity 4. Optional: Catherine the Great *(Offline)*
Instructions

Build a Potemkin village to fool Catherine and her traveling companions.

Grigory Potemkin was a trusted minister to Catherine the Great. He has gone down in history as the man who created "fake" Russian villages along the routes that Catherine traveled.

The Russian serfs were poor and unhappy. Potemkin wanted Catherine and the nobles she traveled with to see happy, prosperous peasants. He chose sites carefully where he was sure Catherine would pass but not stop. He ordered the houses there cleaned up. He even put up some fake fronts of brightly painted homes, churches, barns, and other village buildings. He chose strong, healthy peasants and dressed them in clean, new clothes. He had them stand out in front of their beautiful villages and wave to the passing royals.

Today, if someone tries to fool someone else by presenting a fake scene, we call it a "Potemkin village." Try it yourself. Color the buildings on the Potemkin Village activity sheet. Cut them out and stand them up. Print more than one copy if you'd like more buildings. Do you have toy animals, people, plants, or trees that you can put out front? Would it fool anybody?

ASSESS

Lesson Assessment: Catherine the Great (*Online*)

You will complete an offline assessment covering the main objectives of this lesson. Your learning coach will score this assessment.

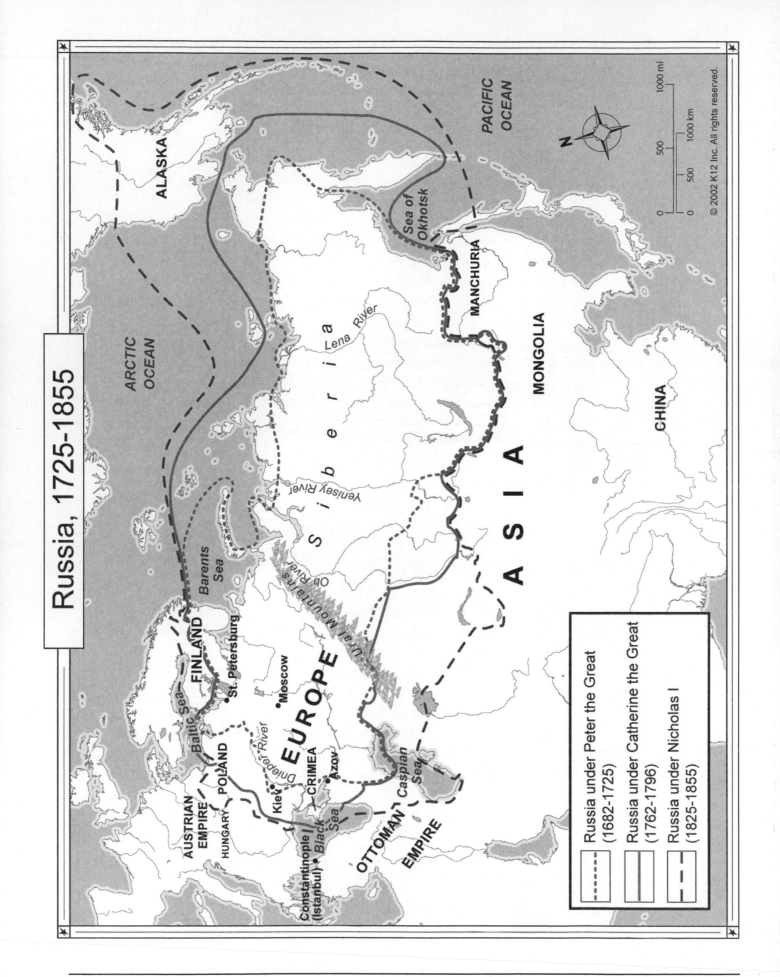

Russia, 1725–1855

ARCTIC OCEAN

ALASKA

PACIFIC OCEAN

Sea of Okhotsk

MANCHURIA

MONGOLIA

CHINA

S i b e r i a

Lena River

Yenisey River

Ob River

Ural Mountains

Barents Sea

FINLAND

St. Petersburg

Baltic Sea

Moscow

EUROPE

POLAND

AUSTRIAN EMPIRE

HUNGARY

Kiev

Dnieper River

CRIMEA

Azov

Black Sea

Constantinople (Istanbul)

OTTOMAN EMPIRE

Caspian Sea

A S I A

N

1000 ml

500

1000 km

500

0

0

Russia under Peter the Great (1682–1725)

Russia under Catherine the Great (1762–1796)

Russia under Nicholas I (1825–1855)

Name

Date

Sea Routes to Southern Russia

On the map, draw trade routes for sailing ships. The routes should start from the Crimean Peninsula in Russia and go to other lands.

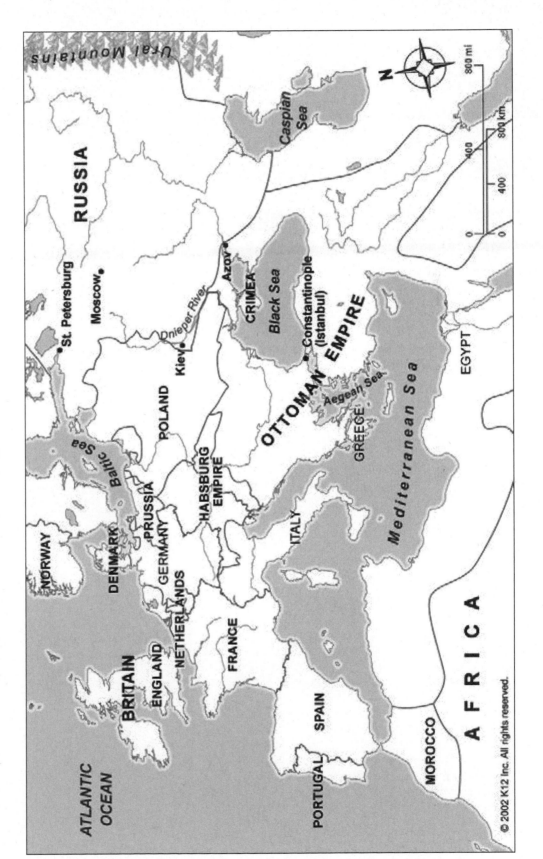

Build a Potemkin Village

First color, then cut out the pieces. Fold the bases so that the fronts of the buildings stand up. Arrange them to present a nice village.

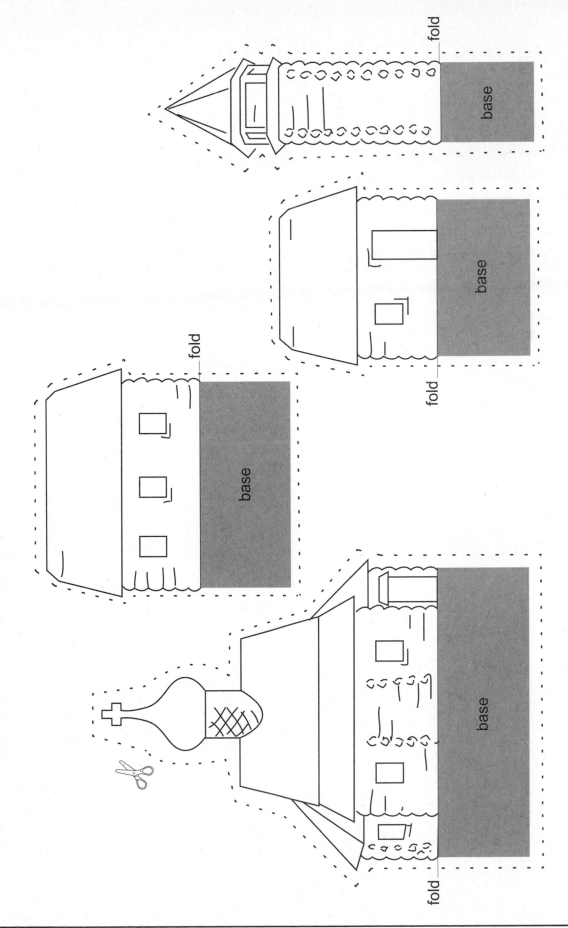

Lesson Assessment

Catherine the Great

1. Catherine the Great was empress of what country? _____

2. True or False: Under Catherine the Great's reign, serfdom grew.

3. True or False: Catherine was against the idea of introducing western ideas to Russia.

4. Which of the following statements is correct?

   Catherine expanded Russia to the Black Sea.
   Catherine lost Russian territory up to the Black Sea.

Student Guide
Lesson 3: Nicholas Nixes Change

Nicholas was czar at a time when new ideas were reaching Russia. People there heard about revolutions in other countries. They heard about republics. They heard about constitutions. Nicholas tried to stop those ideas in Russia and in other countries. For this he was known as "the policeman of Europe."

Lesson Objectives

- Explain that ideas about liberty, revolutions, and constitutions spread to Russia.
- Describe Nicholas as a czar whose reign was harsh, and who was dedicated to stopping the spread of those ideas.
- State that Nicholas was known as "the policeman of Europe."

PREPARE

Approximate lesson time is 60 minutes.

Materials

For the Student

History Journal

🖳 Policeman of Europe Activity Sheet

LEARN
Activity 1: Nicholas Says "No" to Change *(Online)*

Activity 2: History Journal *(Offline)*

Instructions

It's time to add another chapter to the story of the past. Follow the directions to complete a new entry in your History Journal.

Turn to a new page in your History Journal. On this page, write a paragraph that tells what the lesson was about.

Begin with a topic sentence that introduces the paragraph. Include at least three sentences that give details about the lesson. End with a concluding sentence. You may use the Show You Know questions to help you get started.

When you have finished, check your work. Make sure you have written in complete sentences. Check to make sure you used correct capitalization and punctuation. Date your entry and label it with the lesson title.

Guided Learning: Compare your paragraph with the one in the Teacher Guide.

Activity 3: Policeman of Europe *(Offline)*
Instructions

Why was Czar Nicholas I called the "policeman of Europe"? Review by completing the Policeman of Europe activity sheet.

Why was Czar Nicholas I called the "policeman of Europe"? We think of the police as men and women who work to keep us safe from criminals and wrong-doers. They prevent crimes. They capture robbers and murderers. Czar Nicholas I wanted to police the world in a different way. He wanted to stop democratic revolutions and capture revolutionaries!

Police badges are often shaped like a shield. This is a symbol of the role police play in protecting the people. Nicholas believed that he was protecting Russia. What did he feel he was protecting Russia from? How did he go about protecting Russia?

Review today's lesson and answer these questions by completing the Policeman of Europe activity sheet.

Your work will be used as the assessment for this lesson.

ASSESS

Lesson Assessment: Nicholas Nixes Change (*Online*)

Have an adult review your answers to the *Policeman of Europe Activity Sheet*, and input the results online.

Name _____   Date _____

Policeman of Europe

Answer the questions and illustrate the map to support your answers.

1. What kinds of political ideas spread to Russia in the 1800s?

    _____

    Write words for these ideas on the map below. Include arrows showing the spread of these ideas toward Russia.

2. Czar Nicholas was known as the _____ of Europe. Write some words or draw a symbol on the shield that represents Nicholas's views.

3. Describe Nicholas. What did he think about ideas spreading into Russia? What did he decide to do about it? What was his reign like? Draw symbols or write words on the map to show how Nicholas tried to protect Russia.

    _____

    _____

    _____

    _____

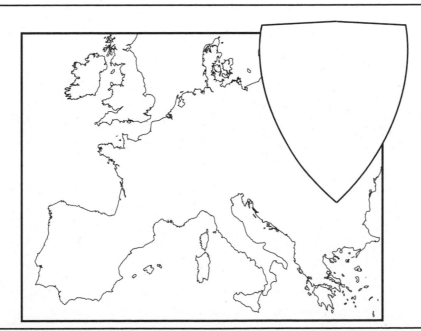

Lesson Assessment

Nicholas Nixes Change

1. What kinds of political ideas spread to Russia in the 1800s? _____

2. Czar Nicholas was known as the _____ of Europe.

3. Describe Nicholas. What did he think about ideas spreading into Russia? What did he decide to do about it? What was his reign like? Draw symbols or write words on the map to show how Nicholas tried to protect Russia.

Student Guide
Lesson 4. Optional: Greece Against the Ottoman Empire

The vast Ottoman Empire ruled many different peoples. The Greeks united to throw off the Ottoman rulers. Greece, the historic home of democracy, became an independent nation in the 1820s.

Lesson Objectives

- Locate the Ottoman Empire, Greece, and the Balkan Peninsula on a map.
- Describe the Ottoman Empire as a vast Muslim empire.
- Explain that the Greeks fought for and won independence from the Ottoman Turks.
- Explain why the Greeks were so proud of their ancient heritage.

PREPARE

Approximate lesson time is 60 minutes.

Materials

> For the Student
>> 🖥 Map of the Ottoman Empire, 1798-1920
>>
>> History Journal
>>
>> 🖥 Greece: Then and Now

Keywords and Pronunciation

Alexander Ypsilanti (uhl-yik-SAHN-dur ip-sih-LAN-tee)

Istanbul (ihs-TAHN-bool)

LEARN
Activity 1. Optional: Optional Lesson Instructions (Online)

Activity 2. Optional: The Ottomans' Unruly Empire (Online)

Print the Ottoman Empire, 1798-1920 map and start the lesson.

Activity 3. Optional: History Journal (Offline)

Instructions

It's time to add another chapter to the story of the past. Follow the directions to complete a new entry in your History Journal.

Turn to a new page in your History Journal. On this page, write a paragraph that tells what the lesson was about.

Begin with a topic sentence that introduces the paragraph. Include at least three sentences that give details about the lesson. End with a concluding sentence. You may use the Show You Know questions to help you get started.

When you have finished, check your work. Make sure you have written in complete sentences. Check to make sure you used correct capitalization and punctuation. Date your entry and label it with the lesson title.

Guided Learning: Compare your paragraph with the one in the Teacher Guide.

Activity 4. Optional: Greece: Then and Now *(Offline)*

Instructions

Use the Greece: Then and Now activity sheet to compare Greece under Ottoman rule with today's Greece.

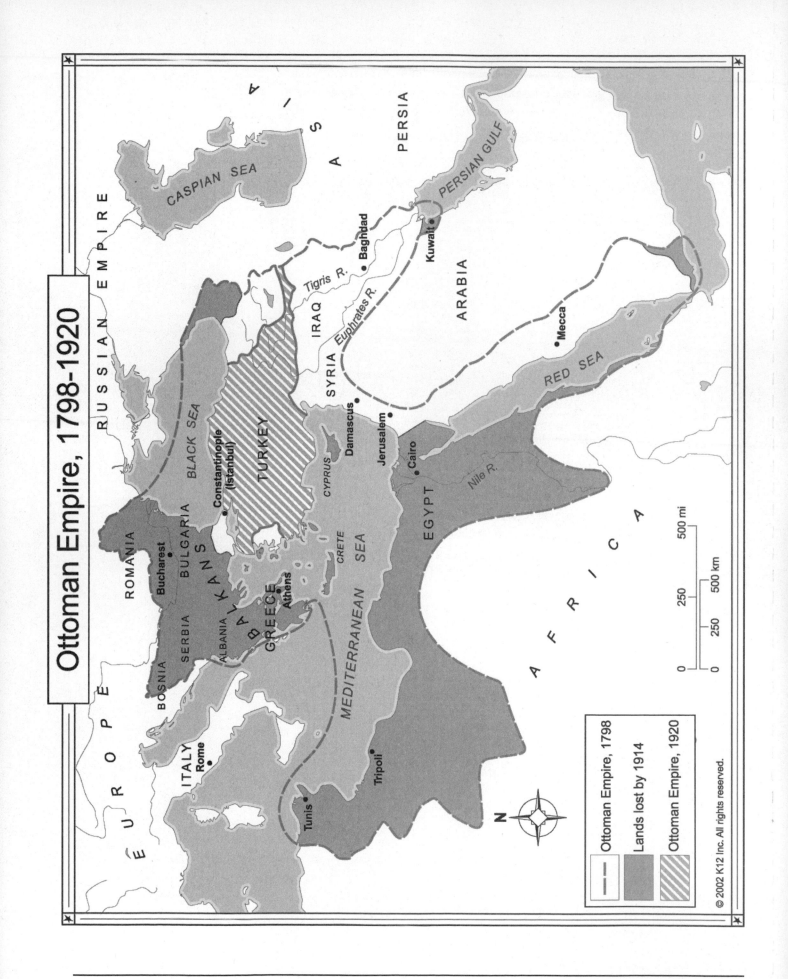

Ottoman Empire, 1798–1920

EUROPE

ASIA

RUSSIAN EMPIRE

CASPIAN SEA

PERSIA

PERSIAN GULF

Tigris R.

Baghdad

Kuwait

ARABIA

Euphrates R.

Mecca

RED SEA

IRAQ

SYRIA

Damascus

Jerusalem

Cairo

Nile R.

EGYPT

BLACK SEA

Constantinople (Istanbul)

TURKEY

CYPRUS

ROMANIA

Bucharest

BULGARIA

B A L K A N S

SERBIA

ALBANIA

GREECE

Athens

CRETE

MEDITERRANEAN SEA

BOSNIA

ITALY

Rome

Tunis

Tripoli

AFRICA

N

Legend	
Ottoman Empire, 1798	
Lands lost by 1914	
Ottoman Empire, 1920	

© 2002 K12 Inc. All rights reserved.

0   250   500 mi
0   250   500 km

Name _____ Date _____

Greece: Then and Now

Then

This flag was used by many Greek forces during the 1821 revolution.
(Color the cross blue.)

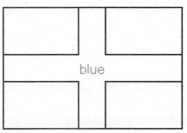

blue

Fill in the blanks with words from the Word Bank to complete the this paragraph.

Greeks lived on the southern tip of the _____ peninsula. They, along

with other people like the Serbs, were ruled by the _____ Empire. This

empire can best be described as a vast _____ empire. Greeks _____

Ottoman rule. Under the Ottomans, Greece had become _____ and

_____ . They were cut off from the rest of _____ . Greeks had to pay

heavy taxes and many were forced into the Ottoman army.

But Greeks were _____ of their ancient heritage. Their ancestors had

given the world many gifts, including _____ . And now, in the early 1800s,

the Greek people wanted to take back power in their own country.

Word Bank

proud	Iberian	Europe	Ottoman	detested	Christian	poor
Balkan	advanced	democracy	enjoyed	Muslim	ashamed	
	North America	Roman	rich	backward		

Greece: Then and Now

Now

The national flag of Greece was adopted on December 22, 1978.
(Color the indicated lines and field behind the cross blue as shown.)

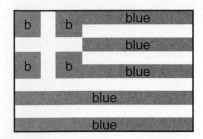

Use a variety of reference materials such as the CIA World Fact Book
(https://www.cia.gov/library/publications/the-world-factbook/) to fill in the missing
information about Greece today.

People   Population (number):

                    Religions Practiced:

                    Languages Spoken:

Government   Year of Independence:

                    Capital:

                    Type of Government:

                    Legal System:

Geography   Bordered By:

                    Land Area (square miles):

                    Climate:

                         Winters:

                         Summers:

                    Elevation Exremes:

                         Lowest Point:

                         Highest Point:

Economy   Type of Economy:

Student Guide
Lesson 5. Optional: The New American Nationalism

In the years after Napoleon's defeat, Americans grew very proud of their democracy and their beautiful country. George Caleb Bingham was an artist who celebrated the American frontier and its great democracy in his paintings.

Lesson Objectives

- Describe Americans as proud of their democracy.
- Explain that Americans were moving west and were enthusiastic about the frontier.
- Describe George Caleb Bingham as an important painter of early American life.
- Characterize Bingham's paintings as filled with admiration for the American landscape, democracy, and people.

PREPARE

Approximate lesson time is 60 minutes.

Materials

For the Student
    History Journal
    paper, 8 1/2" x 11"
    pencils, colored, 16 colors or more

LEARN
Activity 1. Optional: Optional Lesson Instructions (Online)

Activity 2. Optional: George Caleb Bingham Celebrates America (Online)

Activity 3. Optional: History Journal (Offline)
Instructions

It's time to add another chapter to the story of the past. Follow the directions to complete a new entry in your History Journal.

Turn to a new page in your History Journal. On this page, write a paragraph that tells what the lesson was about.

Begin with a topic sentence that introduces the paragraph. Include at least three sentences that give details about the lesson. End with a concluding sentence. You may use the Show You Know questions to help you get started.

When you have finished, check your work. Make sure you have written in complete sentences. Check to make sure you used correct capitalization and punctuation. Date your entry and label it with the lesson title.

Guided Learning: Compare your paragraph with the one in the Teacher Guide.

Activity 4. Optional: A Banner for Democracy *(Online)*
Instructions
Take another look at three of Bingham's paintings. Then create a banner that celebrates democracy.

Activity 5. Optional: The New American Nationalism *(Online)*

Student Guide
Lesson 6: One Nation or Two?

Americans liked their nation's democracy. They liked the way the country was getting bigger. But northern and southern sections of the country had grown up in different ways. As the country expanded, North and South disagreed over the question of slavery.

Lesson Objectives

- Explain that the southern states depended on plantation agriculture and slave labor.
- Explain that the northern states depended mainly on small farms, growing industry, and free labor.
- Explain that the expansion of the United States raised the question of whether slavery should be allowed to expand.

PREPARE

Approximate lesson time is 60 minutes.

Materials

    For the Student

        History Journal

        🖥 Confederate and Union States, 1861

        🖥 Free State or Slave State Activity Sheet

        🖥 Map of Slavery in the U.S., 1850

        The Bushwhacker: A Civil War Adventure by Jennifer Johnson Garrity

Keywords and Pronunciation

Dubuque (duh-BYOOK)

LEARN
Activity 1: A Divided Nation (Online)

Activity 2: History Journal (Offline)

Instructions

It's time to add another chapter to the story of the past. Follow the directions to complete a new entry in your History Journal.

Turn to a new page in your History Journal. On this page, write a paragraph that tells what the lesson was about.

Begin with a topic sentence that introduces the paragraph. Include at least three sentences that give details about the lesson. End with a concluding sentence. You may use the Show You Know questions to help you get started.

When you have finished, check your work. Make sure you have written in complete sentences. Check to make sure you used correct capitalization and punctuation. Date your entry and label it with the lesson title.

Guided Learning: Compare your paragraph with the one in the Teacher Guide.

Activity 3: Free State or Slave State *(Online)*

Create a map that shows which states were free states and which were slave states.

The work you do on this activity sheet will be used to assess how well you understood the lesson.

Activity 4: One Nation or Two? *(Offline)*

Instructions

Check your library or bookstore for *The Bushwhacker: A Civil War Adventure,* by Jennifer Johnson Garrity. Settlers in Missouri found themselves in a difficult position during the Civil War. Missouri was a slave state, but never seceded from the Union. About 100,000 Missourians served in Union armies. Less than half that many, about 40,000, volunteered with Confederate forces. These Confederate sympathizers came to be known as *bushwhackers.*

ASSESS

Lesson Assessment: One Nation or Two? (*Online*)

Have an adult review your answers to the *Free State or Slave State* activity sheet, and input the results online.

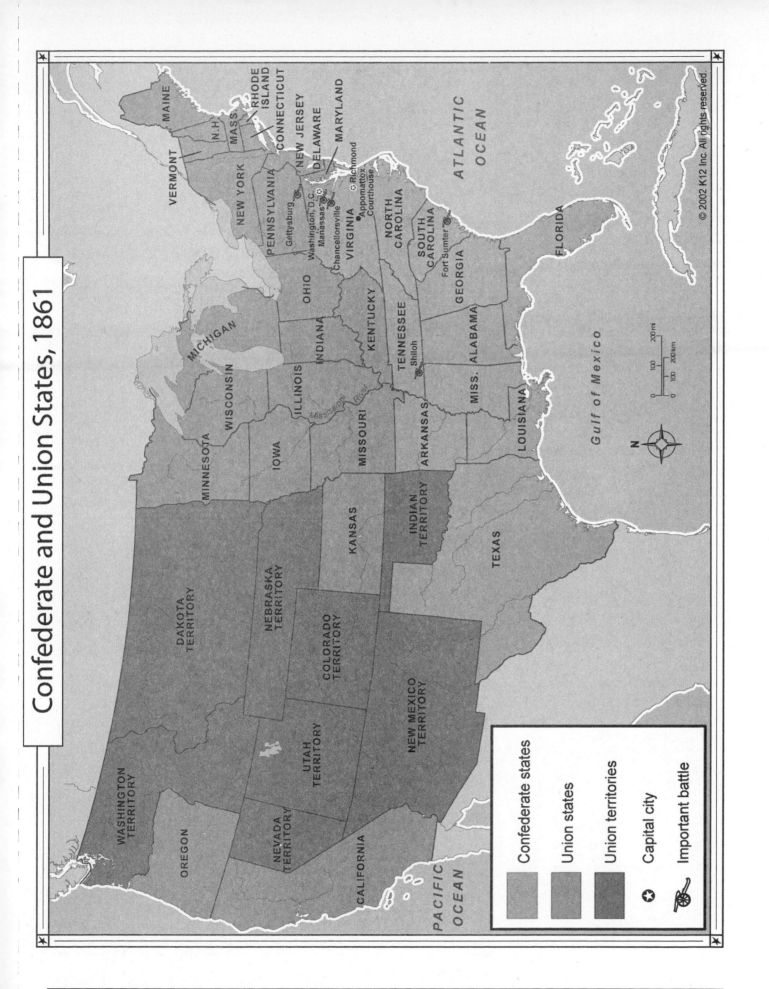

Confederate and Union States, 1861

ATLANTIC OCEAN

MAINE

VERMONT

N.H.

MASS.

RHODE ISLAND

CONNECTICUT

NEW YORK

NEW JERSEY

PENNSYLVANIA

DELAWARE

MARYLAND

Gettysburg

Washington, D.C.

Manassas

Chancellorsville

Richmond

Appomattox Courthouse

VIRGINIA

NORTH CAROLINA

SOUTH CAROLINA

Fort Sumter

GEORGIA

FLORIDA

OHIO

MICHIGAN

INDIANA

KENTUCKY

TENNESSEE

Shiloh

ALABAMA

MISS.

WISCONSIN

ILLINOIS

Mississippi River

IOWA

MINNESOTA

MISSOURI

ARKANSAS

LOUISIANA

Gulf of Mexico

KANSAS

INDIAN TERRITORY

TEXAS

DAKOTA TERRITORY

NEBRASKA TERRITORY

COLORADO TERRITORY

NEW MEXICO TERRITORY

UTAH TERRITORY

WASHINGTON TERRITORY

OREGON

NEVADA TERRITORY

CALIFORNIA

PACIFIC OCEAN

N

200 mi
100
200 km
100
0

Confederate states

Union states

Union territories

Capital city

Important battle

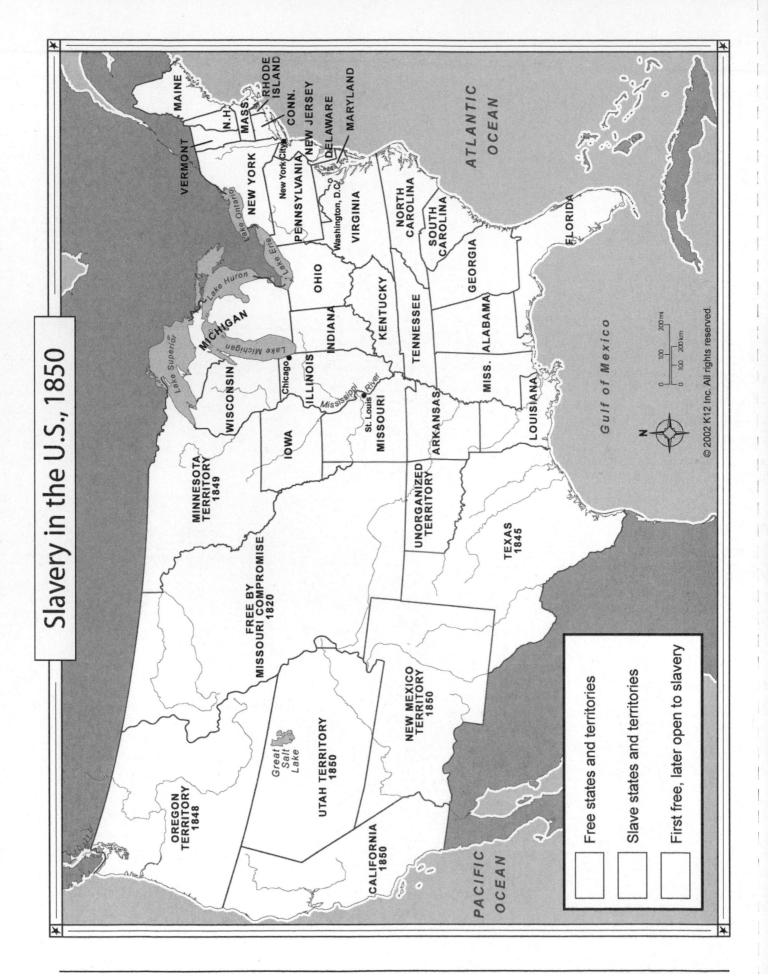

Slavery in the U.S., 1850

MAINE
N.H.
VERMONT
MASS.
RHODE ISLAND
CONN.
NEW YORK
New York City
PENNSYLVANIA
NEW JERSEY
DELAWARE
MARYLAND
Washington, D.C.
VIRGINIA
NORTH CAROLINA
SOUTH CAROLINA
GEORGIA
FLORIDA
OHIO
INDIANA
KENTUCKY
TENNESSEE
ALABAMA
MISS.
MICHIGAN
WISCONSIN
Chicago
ILLINOIS
St. Louis
MISSOURI
ARKANSAS
LOUISIANA
IOWA
Mississippi River
MINNESOTA TERRITORY 1849
FREE BY MISSOURI COMPROMISE 1820
UNORGANIZED TERRITORY
TEXAS 1845
OREGON TERRITORY 1848
UTAH TERRITORY 1850
Great Salt Lake
NEW MEXICO TERRITORY 1850
CALIFORNIA 1850

Lake Superior
Lake Michigan
Lake Huron
Lake Erie
Lake Ontario

ATLANTIC OCEAN

Gulf of Mexico

PACIFIC OCEAN

200 mi
100
200 km
100
0

N

© 2002 K12 Inc. All rights reserved.

Free states and territories

Slave states and territories

First free, later open to slavery

Name _____ Date _____

Free State or Slave State

Print the black-and-white map of Slavery in the U.S.,1850. Use this map to complete this activity sheet. Your answers to questions 1–3 will be assessed.

Use the words and phrases from the word box below for questions 1 and 2.

growing industry	plantation agriculture
small farms slave labor	free labor

1. What did the southern states depend mainly on? List all the phrases that apply.

   _____

   _____

   _____

2. What did the northern states depend mainly on? List all the phrases that apply.

   _____

   _____

   _____

3. Circle the correct answer: As the United States expanded westward, a question was raised. Should settlers be allowed to own (land / slaves / guns / businesses)?

4. Which states were free states and which were slave states? Find out by referring to the color map of the Confederate and Union States, 1861. You can view this map online from the lesson. In the legend, color the box labeled "Union states" a color of your choice. Now color the Union states the same color. Do the same for Union territories and Confederate states, but use different colors.

5. How were the northern and southern regions of the United States different in the years just before the Civil War? How were they alike? Complete the following chart. Write down words and phrases that compare and contrast the North and the South.

Looking at the North and the South	
North	South

Lesson Assessment

One Nation or Two?

Use the words and phrases from the word box below for questions 1 and 2.

growing industry	plantation agriculture	
small farms	slave labor	free labor

1. What did the southern states depend mainly on? List all the phrases that apply.
   _____

2. What did the northern states depend mainly on? List all the phrases that apply.
   _____

3. Circle the correct answer: As the United States expanded westward, a question was raised. Should settlers be allowed to own (land / slaves / guns / businesses)?

Student Guide
Lesson 7: The Civil War Makes One Nation

Would the United States continue to exist as a single nation? Would slavery spread and continue? The Civil War answered those questions. It was America's bloodiest conflict, but it ended slavery and ensured that the United States would be one nation.

Lesson Objectives

- Describe the expansion of slavery into the new territories as the issue that divided North from South.
- Explain that after Abraham Lincoln was elected president, several southern states seceded from the Union.
- Describe the Civil War as America's bloodiest war.
- Describe the Civil War as the war that ended slavery and confirmed that the United States was a single nation.

PREPARE

Approximate lesson time is 60 minutes.

Materials

For the Student

History Journal

- Map of Confederate and Union States, 1861 (b/w)
- Map of Confederate and Union States, 1861 (color)
- Mapping the Civil War Activity Sheet

Keywords and Pronunciation

Manassas (muh-NA-suhs)

secede : To withdraw from an organization.

Ulysses (you-LIH-seez)

LEARN
Activity 1: One Nation (Online)

Activity 2: History Journal (Offline)

Instructions

It's time to add another chapter to the story of the past. Follow the directions to complete a new entry in your History Journal.

Turn to a new page in your History Journal. On this page, write a paragraph that tells what the lesson was about.

Begin with a topic sentence that introduces the paragraph. Include at least three sentences that give details about the lesson. End with a concluding sentence. You may use the Show You Know questions to help you get started.

When you have finished, check your work. Make sure you have written in complete sentences. Check to make sure you used correct capitalization and punctuation. Date your entry and label it with the lesson title.

Guided Learning: Compare your paragraph with the one in the Teacher Guide.

Activity 3: Mapping the Civil War (Online)

Instructions

Map important locations and events of the Civil War on the Mapping the Civil War activity sheet. To complete this activity, you will need to print the map of Confederate and Union States, 1861 (b/w) and view the color version of this map

Activity 4. Optional: The Civil War Makes One Nation (Online)

ASSESS

Lesson Assessment: The Civil War Makes One Nation (Online)

You will complete an offline assessment covering the main objectives of this lesson. Your learning coach will score this assessment.

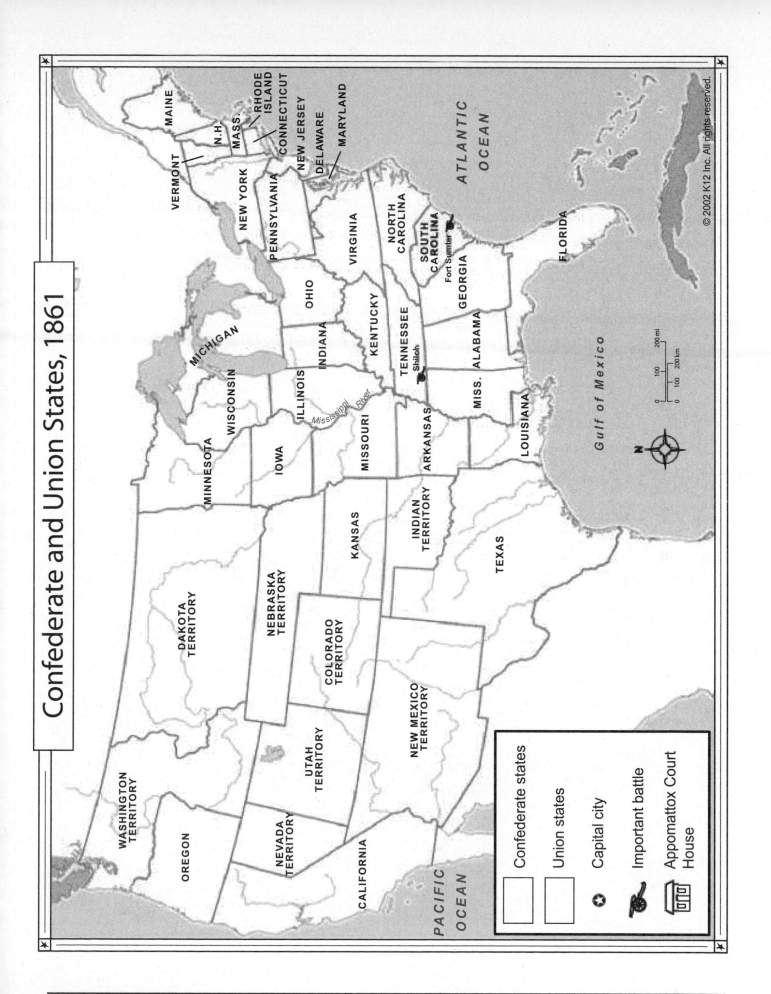

Confederate and Union States, 1861

MAINE

RHODE ISLAND

N.H.

MASS.

CONNECTICUT

NEW JERSEY

DELAWARE

MARYLAND

VERMONT

NEW YORK

PENNSYLVANIA

VIRGINIA

NORTH CAROLINA

SOUTH CAROLINA

Fort Sumter

GEORGIA

ATLANTIC OCEAN

FLORIDA

MICHIGAN

OHIO

INDIANA

KENTUCKY

TENNESSEE

Shiloh

ALABAMA

MISS.

ILLINOIS

Mississippi River

WISCONSIN

MINNESOTA

IOWA

MISSOURI

ARKANSAS

LOUISIANA

Gulf of Mexico

DAKOTA TERRITORY

NEBRASKA TERRITORY

KANSAS

INDIAN TERRITORY

TEXAS

COLORADO TERRITORY

NEW MEXICO TERRITORY

UTAH TERRITORY

WASHINGTON TERRITORY

OREGON

NEVADA TERRITORY

CALIFORNIA

PACIFIC OCEAN

200 mi

100   200 km

100

0   0

N

Legend

Confederate states

Union states

Capital city

Important battle

Appomattox Court House

© 2002 K12 Inc. All rights reserved.

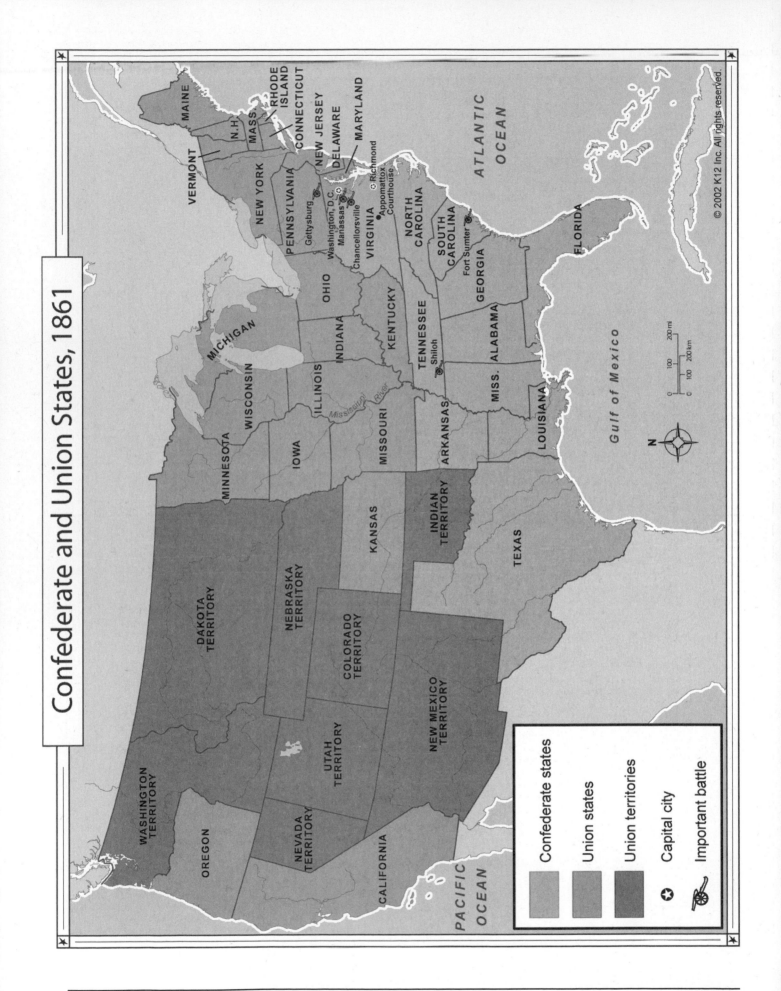

Confederate and Union States, 1861

ATLANTIC OCEAN

MAINE

N.H.

MASS.

RHODE ISLAND

CONNECTICUT

NEW JERSEY

MARYLAND

DELAWARE

VERMONT

NEW YORK

PENNSYLVANIA

Washington, D.C.

Gettysburg

Manassas

Chancellorsville

Appomattox Courthouse

Richmond

VIRGINIA

NORTH CAROLINA

SOUTH CAROLINA

Fort Sumter

GEORGIA

FLORIDA

OHIO

INDIANA

KENTUCKY

TENNESSEE

Shiloh

ALABAMA

MISS.

LOUISIANA

MICHIGAN

WISCONSIN

ILLINOIS

Mississippi River

MINNESOTA

IOWA

MISSOURI

ARKANSAS

KANSAS

INDIAN TERRITORY

TEXAS

Gulf of Mexico

DAKOTA TERRITORY

NEBRASKA TERRITORY

COLORADO TERRITORY

NEW MEXICO TERRITORY

WASHINGTON TERRITORY

OREGON

UTAH TERRITORY

NEVADA TERRITORY

CALIFORNIA

PACIFIC OCEAN

N

200 mi

200 km

100

100

0

0

Legend:

Confederate states

Union states

Union territories

Capital city

Important battle

Name _____   Date _____

Mapping the Civil War

1. Color the Union states blue. Color the appropriate box in the legend blue.

2. Color the Confederate states gray. Color the appropriate box in the legend gray.

3. Draw a bold red line to represent the border between northern and southern states.

4. Show the locations of the following:

    ·   Washington, D.C.
    ·   Richmond (capital of the Confederacy)
    ·   Battle of Gettysburg (one of the most important battles in the war)
    ·   Battle of Manassas (first major land battle of the war)
    ·   Fort Sumter, Charleston, South Carolina (where the Civil War began)
    ·   Village of Appomattox Court House (where the Civil War ended)

5. What issue divided North from South?

    _____

    _____

6. What did several southern states do after Abraham Lincoln was elected president?

    _____

    _____

Mapping the Civil War

7. Which of the following three-word phrases best describes the Civil War?

America's shortest war

America's longest war

America's bloodiest war

America's first war

8. What two things did the Civil War do? Choose two from the following list.

It made slavery legal in all western states.

It ended slavery.

It made plantations larger.

It confirmed that the United States was a single nation.

It made several northern states secede from the Union.

Guided Learning: Check your answers to questions 5–8 with those in the Teacher Guide.

Lesson Assessment

The Civil War Makes One Nation

1. What issue divided the North from the South? _____

2. What did several southern states do after Abraham Lincoln was elected president? _____

3. How would you describe the Civil War? _____

4. What effect did the Civil War have on slavery? _____

5. Did the Civil War confirm that the United States was a group of many states? Or did it confirm that it was a single nation? _____

Student Guide
Lesson 8: Lincoln's Leadership

Abraham Lincoln worked to make sure the United States of America remained one nation. He also helped Americans think about what their country stood for. He helped them understand that the terrible Civil War might result in "a new birth of freedom."

Lesson Objectives

- Identify Abraham Lincoln as president of the United States during the Civil War.
- Describe Lincoln as a man committed to saving the Union.
- Explain that Lincoln hoped the Civil War would bring about a "new birth of freedom" in the United States by ending slavery.
- Describe the Gettysburg Address as an important speech given by Lincoln during the Civil War.

PREPARE

Approximate lesson time is 60 minutes.

Materials

For the Student

History Journal

⌨ Gettysburg Address

LEARN
Activity 1: Abraham Lincoln *(Online)*

Activity 2: Lincoln's Speechwriter *(Offline)*
Instructions

Lincoln wrote the Gettysburg Address himself. But imagine you were asked to write the speech for him. Abraham Lincoln wrote the speech that would become known as the Gettysburg Address. Today, presidents hire speechwriters to write the speeches they give. Imagine you are Abraham Lincoln's speechwriter. To gather material for the Gettysburg Address speech, you've interviewed Lincoln and asked him a series of questions.

Here are the questions. In your History Journal, write the number for each question. Then write the answer you think Lincoln would have given.

---

1. Mr. Lincoln, what happened a little less than one hundred years ago that you want to preserve?
2. What promises did the writers of the Declaration of Independence talk about that you believe the nation may not have lived up to?
3. What do you think the Civil War is a test for?
4. What do you think the Union soldiers who died at Gettysburg died for? Why did they fight?
5. Who do you think should dedicate and consecrate the Gettysburg battlefield?
6. What should the people who are still alive dedicate themselves to?
7. What should not disappear from the world?

Guided Learning: Check your answers against the ones in the Teacher Guide.

ASSESS

Lesson Assessment: Lincoln's Leadership (*Online*)

You will complete an online assessment covering the main objectives of this lesson. Your assessment will be scored by the computer.

LEARN

Activity 3. Optional: Lincoln's Leadership (*Offline*)

Instructions

Memorize and recite one of the greatest speeches ever made on American soil.

Gettysburg Address

Four score and seven years ago, our fathers brought forth upon this continent a new nation, conceived in liberty, and dedicated to the proposition that all men are created equal.

Now we are engaged in a great civil war, testing whether that nation, or any nation so conceived and so dedicated, can long endure. We are met on a great battlefield of that war. We have come to dedicate a portion of that field, as a final resting place for those who here gave their lives that that nation might live. It is altogether fitting and proper that we should do this.

But, in a larger sense, we cannot dedicate—we cannot consecrate—we cannot hallow—this ground. The brave men, living and dead, who struggled here, have consecrated it, far above our poor power to add or detract. The world will little note, nor long remember what we say here, but it can never forget what they did here. It is for us the living, rather, to be dedicated here to the unfinished work which they who fought here have thus far so nobly advanced. It is rather for us to be here dedicated to the great task remaining before us—that from these honored dead we take increased devotion to that cause for which they gave the last full measure of devotion—that we here highly resolve that these dead shall not have died in vain—that this nation, under God, shall have a new birth of freedom—and that government of the people, by the people, for the people, shall not perish from the earth.

Abraham Lincoln
November 19, 1863

Student Guide
Lesson 9: The Brothers Grimm in Germany

In 1815, the land we call "Germany" was divided into many different kingdoms. These kingdoms shared the German language but little else. The Brothers Grimm collected German folktales to help Germans think of themselves as one people.

Lesson Objectives

- Describe nineteenth-century Germany as a land made of many different kingdoms.
- Explain that the German language was the main common bond of these kingdoms.
- Recognize that the Brothers Grimm wanted to promote a sense of national identity and pride.
- Explain that the Brothers Grimm collected German folktales.

PREPARE

Approximate lesson time is 60 minutes.

Materials

> For the Student
>> 🖳 Map of German Kingdoms, 1815
>> History Journal

Keywords and Pronunciation

Albrecht Dürer (AHL-brekt DYOUR-ur)

folktale : A story or fairy tale that belongs to a certain land.

Frau Viehmann (frow FEE-mahn)

Jacob and Wilhelm Grimm (YAH-kub and VIL-helm grim)

Johannes Gutenberg (yoh-HAHN-uhs GOOT-n-burg)

LEARN
Activity 1: A Germany for Germans? *(Online)*

Once upon a time, not so long ago, the Brothers Grimm set out to collect German folk tales. Germany as a nation did not exist at the time. These stories helped to bring the people of the German states together.

Activity 2: History Journal *(Offline)*

Instructions

It's time to add another chapter to the story of the past. Follow the directions to complete a new entry in your History Journal.

Turn to a new page in your History Journal. On this page, write a paragraph that tells what the lesson was about. Your work will be used to assess how well you understood the lesson.

Begin with a topic sentence that introduces the paragraph. Include at least three sentences that give details about the lesson. End with a concluding sentence. You may use the Show You Know questions to help you get started.

You should include the answers to these questions in your paragraph.

1. Germany of the 1800s was a land made of _____.
2. What was the main common bond that united the German people?
3. How did the Brothers Grimm want Germans to think of themselves?
4. What did the Brothers Grimm collect?

When you have finished, check your work. Make sure you have written in complete sentences. Check to make sure you used correct capitalization and punctuation. Date your entry and label it with the lesson title.

Guided Learning: Compare your paragraph with the one in the Teacher Guide.

Activity 3: Collecting Tales (Offline)

Instructions

In the 1800s, Germany was a land made up of many different kingdoms. The German language was the main common bond of these kingdoms. The Brothers Grimm wanted to promote a sense of national identity and pride. One way in which they did this was to collect German folktales.

Now it's time for you to collect these tales. Using the Internet, or by visiting your library, write down the titles of as many Brothers Grimm fairy tales as you can. Challenge a friend or an adult to see who can find the most titles.

After your list is complete:

1. Circle all the titles you have read.

2. Underline the titles you've never heard of.

3. Star your favorite.

Activity 4. Optional: The Brothers Grimm in Germany (Offline)

Instructions

Choose one of these two activities. Or, if you'd like, do them both.

Here are two activities. Choose one, or do them both!

1. Do you have a favorite fairy tale? If you do, there's a good chance it's based on a German folktale collected by Jacob and Wilhelm Grimm hundreds of years ago. What about a parent or an older relative? Do you think they have a favorite? Find out! See if you can get someone to tell you their favorite fairy tale. It might be interesting to hear how they tell the story.

2. Go to the library and try to find a Grimm's fairy tale you've never heard before. Check it out. Maybe you can read the story to a younger brother, sister, or friend.

ASSESS

Lesson Assessment: The Brothers Grimm in Germany (Online)

Have an adult review your answers to the History Journal activity, and input the results online.

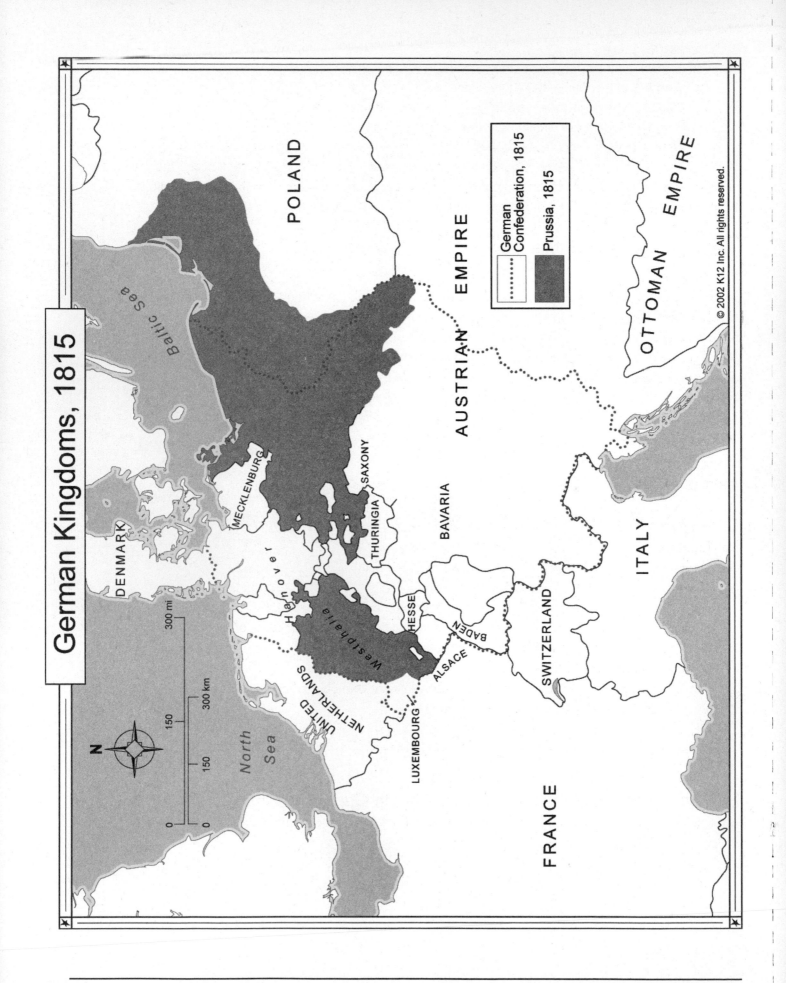

German Kingdoms, 1815

POLAND

AUSTRIAN EMPIRE

OTTOMAN EMPIRE

German Confederation, 1815

Prussia, 1815

Baltic Sea

MECKLENBURG

SAXONY

THURINGIA

BAVARIA

DENMARK

Hanover

Westphalia

HESSE

BADEN

ALSACE

SWITZERLAND

ITALY

North Sea

UNITED NETHERLANDS

LUXEMBOURG

FRANCE

N

300 mi

300 km

150

150

0

0

Name _____   Date _____

Lesson Assessment

The Brothers Grimm in Germany

1. Germany of the 1800s was a land made of _____.

2. What was the main common bond that united the German people?_____

3. How did the Brothers Grimm want Germans to think of themselves?_____

4. What did the Brothers Grimm collect?_____

Student Guide
Lesson 10: Bismarck Unites Germany

The land we now call "Germany" was once many kingdoms. A man named Otto von Bismarck changed that. He united Germany into a single nation. He did it by force--by "blood and iron."

Lesson Objectives

- Recall that Germany was made up of many kingdoms.
- Describe Prussia as the most powerful German kingdom.
- Identify Otto von Bismarck as a Prussian statesman who united Germany into a single nation.
- Describe Bismarck as a man who believed in using "blood and iron" to settle tough problems.

PREPARE

Approximate lesson time is 60 minutes.

Materials

For the Student

    💻 Map of German Kingdoms, 1815-1871

    History Journal

    💻 The Iron Chancellor Activity Sheet

Keywords and Pronunciation

chancellor : the title for the head of government in some countries

confederation : A group of states or kingdoms that are allied with each other.

Otto von Bismarck (AHT-oh fawn BIZ-mahrk)

prime minister : The title for the head of government in some countries.

LEARN
Activity 1: Man With a Mission *(Online)*

Activity 2: History Journal *(Offline)*

Instructions

It's time to add another chapter to the story of the past. Follow the directions to complete a new entry in your History Journal.

Turn to a new page in your History Journal. On this page, write a paragraph that tells what the lesson was about.

Begin with a topic sentence that introduces the paragraph. Include at least three sentences that give details about the lesson. End with a concluding sentence. You may use the Show You Know questions to help you get started.

When you have finished, check your work. Make sure you have written in complete sentences. Check to make sure you used correct capitalization and punctuation. Date your entry and label it with the lesson title.

Guided Learning: Compare your paragraph with the one in the Teacher Guide.

Activity 3: The Iron Chancellor *(Offline)*
Instructions
Print and complete the Iron Chancellor activity sheet.

ASSESS
Lesson Assessment: Bismark Unites Germany (*Online*)
Have an adult review your answers to *The Iron Chancellor* activity sheet, and input the results online.

Name _____   Date _____

The Iron Chancellor

1. Germany was made up of _____ kingdoms.

2. The most powerful German kingdom was _____ .

3. A statesman named _____ united Germany into a single nation.

4. The Prussian statesman believed in using _____ to settle tough problems.

5. Explain briefly why Bismarck wanted a war between Prussia and France.

_____

_____

Word Box

many   peaceful negotiation   Westphalia   one
Otto von Bismarck   blood and iron   Peter the Great   Prussia

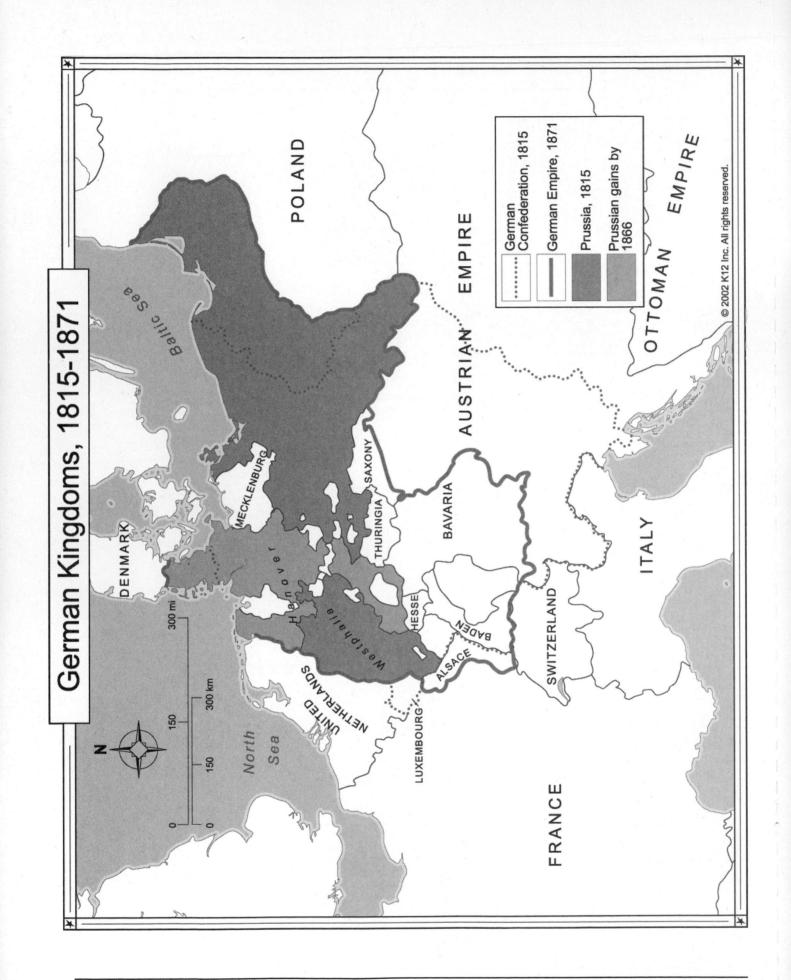

German Kingdoms, 1815–1871

POLAND

AUSTRIAN EMPIRE

OTTOMAN EMPIRE

Legend:
- German Confederation, 1815
- German Empire, 1871
- Prussia, 1815
- Prussian gains by 1866

© 2002 K12 Inc. All rights reserved.

Baltic Sea

DENMARK

MECKLENBURG

SAXONY

THURINGIA

Hanover

Westphalia

HESSE

BAVARIA

BADEN

ALSACE

LUXEMBOURG

UNITED NETHERLANDS

SWITZERLAND

ITALY

FRANCE

North Sea

N

300 mi

300 km

150

150

300

0

0

Lesson Assessment

Bismarck Unites Germany

1. Germany was made up of _____ kingdoms.

2. The most powerful German kingdom was _____.

3. A statesman named _____ united Germany into a single nation.

4. The Prussian statesman believed in using _____to settle tough problems.

5. Explain briefly why Bismarck wanted a war between Prussia and France.

Student Guide
Lesson 11: Garibaldi Fights for a United Italy

Giuseppe Garibaldi worked hard to unite the Italian peninsula into a single nation. This hero really loved Italy.

Lesson Objectives

- Explain that Italy was once divided into many city-states and kingdoms.
- Describe Giuseppe Garibaldi as a military leader who fought to unite Italy.
- Identify the Red Shirts as the name of Garibaldi's army.
- Explain that Italy became a single nation.

PREPARE

Approximate lesson time is 60 minutes.

Materials

For the Student

🖳 Map of Italy, 1815-1870

History Journal

Keywords and Pronunciation

Alexandre Dumas (ahl-uhks-AHN-druh dyoo-MAH)
Cincinnatus (sin-sih-NAT-uhs)
Giuseppe Garibaldi (joo-ZEP-pay gah-ree-BAHL-dee)
Viva Garibaldi (VEE-vah gah-ree-BAHL-dee)

LEARN
Activity 1: The Making of Italy *(Online)*

Activity 2: History Journal *(Offline)*
Instructions

It's time to add another chapter to the story of the past. Follow the directions to complete a new entry in your History Journal.

Turn to a new page in your History Journal. On this page, write a paragraph that tells what the lesson was about.

Begin with a topic sentence that introduces the paragraph. Include at least three sentences that give details about the lesson. End with a concluding sentence. You may use the Show You Know questions to help you get started.

When you have finished, check your work. Make sure you have written in complete sentences. Check to make sure you used correct capitalization and punctuation. Date your entry and label it with the lesson title.

Guided Learning: Compare your paragraph with the one in the Teacher Guide.

Activity 3: Wanted: A United Italy (Offline)

Instructions

Create a poster that tries to get people to join Garibaldi's army - the Red Shirts.

Create a recruiting poster that Garibaldi might have used to get people to join his army, the Red Shirts.

You must somehow include the following facts in your poster:

- Italy was once divided into many city-states and kingdoms
- Giuseppe Garibaldi is leading the fight to unify Italy
- Garibaldi's army is called the Red Shirts

The following websites provide examples of recruiting posters. You can use these examples to help you design your poster.

- 4th Texas Recruiting Poster
- Recruiting Poster
- Recruiting Poster for the 1st and 2nd NC Union Volunteers
- 15th MVI Recruiting Poster

ASSESS

Lesson Assessment: Bismarck Unites Germany (Online)

You will complete an online assessment covering the main objectives of this lesson. Your assessment will be scored by the computer.

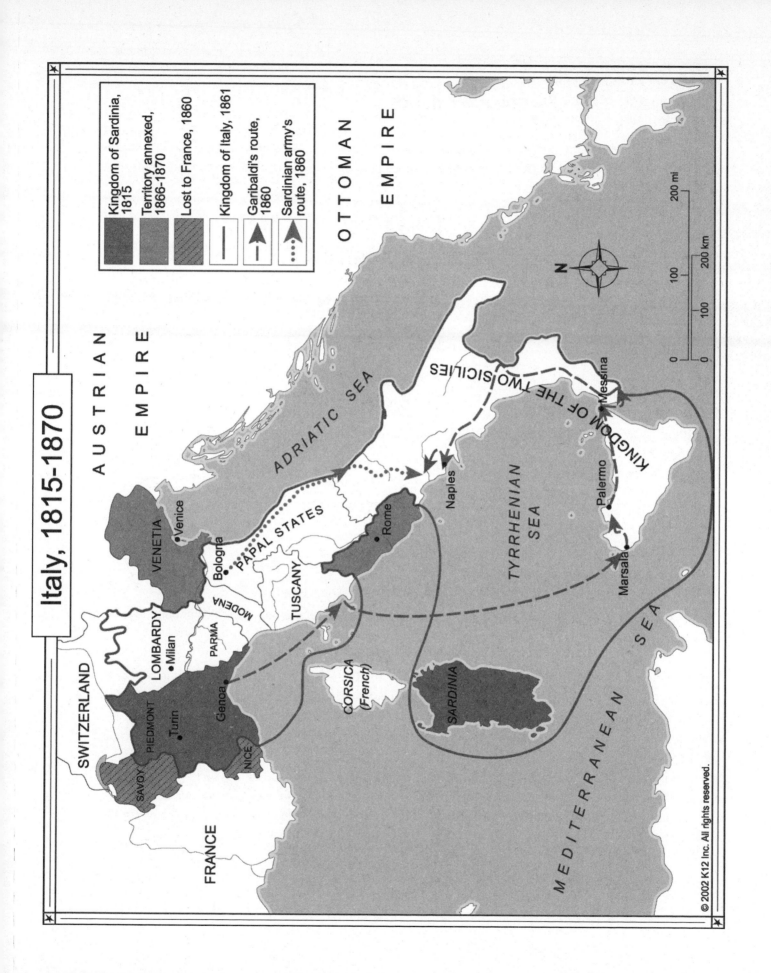

Italy, 1815-1870

Kingdom of Sardinia, 1815

Territory annexed, 1866-1870

Lost to France, 1860

Kingdom of Italy, 1861

Garibaldi's route, 1860

Sardinian army's route, 1860

AUSTRIAN EMPIRE

OTTOMAN EMPIRE

SWITZERLAND

FRANCE

VENETIA

Venice

LOMBARDY

Milan

PIEDMONT

Turin

SAVOY

NICE

Genoa

MODENA

PARMA

Bologna

PAPAL STATES

TUSCANY

Rome

CORSICA (French)

SARDINIA

ADRIATIC SEA

TYRRHENIAN SEA

MEDITERRANEAN SEA

KINGDOM OF THE TWO SICILIES

Naples

Messina

Palermo

Marsala

N

0   100   200 km

0   100   200 mi

© 2002 K12 Inc. All rights reserved.

Student Guide
Lesson 12: The Olympics Revived

As nationalism grew, some people wanted to see athletic competition between countries. The Olympic Games were reborn in 1896. Pierre de Coubertin is remembered as the father of the modern Olympic Games.

Lesson Objectives

- Recall that the modern Olympic Games had their origin in ancient Greece.
- Describe Baron de Coubertin as the father of the modern Olympic Games.
- State that the first modern Olympic Games were held in Athens.
- Describe the Olympics as international athletic competitions and a way for nations to compete peacefully.

PREPARE

Approximate lesson time is 60 minutes.

Keywords and Pronunciation

Demetrius Vikelas (duh-MEE-tree-uhs vee-KEH-luhs)

drachmas (DRAK-muhs)

Pierre de Coubertin (pyehr duh koo-behr-tan)

LEARN
Activity 1: The First Modern Olympics *(Online)*

Activity 2. Optional: Vikelas Writes Persuasively *(Offline)*

What might Demetrius Vikelas have written to persuade the world that the new Olympics should be held in Greece?

Imagine you are Demetrius Vikelas, the chairman of the 1896 International Olympic Committee. Pierre de Coubertin's idea to revive the Olympics, and make them international competitions, has finally been accepted by most countries. Now the International Olympic Committee must select a location for the first "new" Olympics. Write a persuasive letter to convince the committee that the first games of the revived Olympics should be held in Greece.

When you write persuasively, you try to convince people to think the way you do. To be persuasive, state your opinion clearly. Then use facts, personal experiences, and explanations to back up your opinion.

In your letter, include the answer to this question: Why did many people think reviving the Olympics was a good idea?

ASSESS

Lesson Assessment: The Olympics Revived (*Online*)

You will complete an online assessment covering the main objectives of this lesson. Your assessment will be scored by the computer.

LEARN

Activity 3. Optional: The Olympics Revived (*Offline*)

Get together with some friends and compete in your own Olympics.

About 300 athletes competed in the 1896 Olympic Games. Some 230 of them were Greek. The remaining athletes represented twelve other countries. They competed in 43 events. The program included the following sports: fencing, gymnastics, swimming, tennis, track and field, cycling, weightlifting, wrestling, and shooting. Select two or three events, gather some friends, and have your own Olympics. If you choose the right events, you can do this in your backyard.

In the 1896 Olympics, athletes participated in the 100 meter race, the hop, step, and jump, and the discus throw. You could shorten the race to a dash and use a Frisbee as a discus. As far as the hop, step, and jump goes (also called the triple jump) -- you'll need to hop onto the Internet and find out how to perform this event!

Student Guide
Lesson 13: Unit Review and Assessment

You've completed this unit, and now it's time to review what you've learned and take the unit assessment.

Lesson Objectives

- Demonstrate mastery of important knowledge and skills in this unit.
- Describe Peter the Great as a czar who tried to bring western ways to Russia.
- Explain that ideas about liberty, revolutions, and constitutions spread to Russia.
- Describe Nicholas as a czar whose reign was harsh, and who was dedicated to stopping the spread of those ideas.
- State that Nicholas was known as "the policeman of Europe."
- Explain that the southern states depended on plantation agriculture and slave labor.
- Explain that the northern states depended mainly on small farms, growing industry, and free labor.
- Describe the expansion of slavery into the new territories as the issue that divided North from South.
- Explain that after Abraham Lincoln was elected president, several southern states seceded from the Union.
- Describe the Civil War as the war that ended slavery and confirmed that the United States was a single nation.
- Identify Abraham Lincoln as president of the United States during the Civil War.
- Describe the Gettysburg Address as an important speech given by Lincoln during the Civil War.
- Describe nineteenth-century Germany as a land made of many different kingdoms.
- Explain that the German language was the main common bond of these kingdoms.
- Recognize that the Brothers Grimm wanted to promote a sense of national identity and pride.
- Describe Prussia as the most powerful German kingdom.
- Identify Otto von Bismarck as a Prussian statesman who united Germany into a single nation.
- Explain that Italy was once divided into many city-states and kingdoms.
- Describe Giuseppe Garibaldi as a military leader who fought to unite Italy.
- Explain that Italy became a single nation.
- Recall that the modern Olympic Games had their origin in ancient Greece.
- Describe the Olympics as international athletic competitions and a way for nations to compete peacefully.
- Explain that Catherine the Great expanded Russia to the Black Sea.
- Describe nationalism as a strong sense of pride in one's nation.
- Identify key figures and events that promoted nationalism (Ypsilanti, Lincoln, U.S. Civil War, Brothers Grimm, Bismarck, Garibaldi).
- Explain that the first modern Olympics began in the late 1800s with the growth of nationalism.

PREPARE

Approximate lesson time is 60 minutes.

LEARN

Activity 1: The Growth of Nations (Offline)

Instructions

We've covered a lot, and now it's time to take a look back. Here's what you should remember about the growth of nations.

Long ago, when castles dotted hillsides and knights rode brightly clad horses, people didn't think about being part of a nation. Their world was only as big as their lord's manor. And there were many lords and manors-lots of nobles, princes, and bishops-as well as many little states.

But in time, that changed. Strong kings and queens began to unite their lands. People became attached not just to the speck of land they farmed, but to their country. They became attached to countries such as England, Germany, or the United States of America.

In the period of history we've just studied, nations seemed to burst forth. Strong monarchs and leaders helped the process along.

Think about Russia. The Russian leader's title tells you he was strong and powerful. What were Russian monarchs called? (Hint: the title means caesar.) [1]

One great Russian czar wanted to learn everything he could from western Europe. He traveled to Holland and studied there. He was fascinated by the Scientific Revolution. He dreamed of making Russia a great western nation. What was that czar's name? [2]

Peter the Great built a new western-style capital at St. Petersburg and introduced many new ideas to Russians. Other Russian leaders tried to follow Peter's example. Which German princess became a Russian empress and tried to bring more of the west to Russia? [3]

Catherine the Great expanded industry and won great military victories for her beloved Russia. During her reign, Russia also conquered a peninsula called the Crimea. What sea surrounds the Crimea? [4]

Now Russian ships could sail easily from the Black Sea to the Mediterranean. They could trade more easily with the West. Catherine hoped this new trade route would help Russia become a great industrial power.

But something stood in the way. Most of the Russian people were peasants who were forced to work the land for noble lords. What were those peasants called? [5]

Serfs could be bought and sold with the land. Would there ever be a time when serfs would be free to live and work where they wanted? Not while Catherine was empress. Freeing the serfs did not occur to her.

It did occur to the czars who followed Catherine. Their names were Alexander and then Nicholas. But then they saw the bloodshed in France during the French Revolution. They saw Napoleon march into Russia. After that, the czars decided that liberty, revolutions, and constitutions posed big risks.

Czar Nicholas believed his job was to keep order. So he kept the serfs tied to the land and vowed to stop all revolutions. What was Czar Nicholas's nickname? [6]

Maybe Nicholas could stop some revolutions, but he couldn't stop them everywhere. To the south of Russia, an aging empire was losing its grip. Which Muslim empire ruled the Balkans, Asia Minor, and other parts of Asia? [7]

Which people launched a revolutionary movement against the Ottomans? [8]

Ancient times had been a period of glory for the Greeks. They gave the world democracy, philosophy, the Olympic Games, and great literature. Now the Greeks watched the American Revolution and then the French Revolution. More and more people talked about self-rule and the rights of man. The Greeks began to ask themselves: Why should we, the inventors of democracy, be ruled by the Ottomans? Ypsilanti led a revolution, and by 1830 the modern nation of Greece was born.

Americans were enthusiastic about the Greek revolution. The Americans had started their republic with a revolution in 1776. It was a bold democratic experiment. By the 1800s the French Revolution had failed, but the young United States was thriving. Americans were electing their own leaders. They were building canals and railroads. They were pushing west. People were proud of their country.

But what did it mean to be an American? Most people knew it had something to do with democracy and freedom. But democracy and freedom for whom? In the South, owners of large plantations needed lots of labor. How did they get it? [9]

Slaves had been imported from Africa at first. Then descendants of those Africans were kept as slaves. They were forced to live and work the plantations. Meanwhile, in the North, slavery had almost died out. Who provided the labor there? [10]

Americans began to ask some important questions. Should slavery spread to the new western territories? What kind of nation would the United States be? Half-slave? Half-free? Or no nation at all? It took a civil war to settle those questions.

In 1860, Americans elected as president a lawyer from Illinois. He had spoken out against allowing slavery to spread west. What was his name? [11]

When Lincoln became president, the Southern states decided they did not want to be part of the United States any longer. What did they do? [12]

A civil war began. Lincoln started out by saying it was a war to save the Union. He ended up by saying it was a war for "a new birth of freedom." In which famous speech did Lincoln explain his hopes about the war? [13]

The Civil War was the deadliest war the United States ever fought. When it ended, however, the nation was one country. It was a union again, and slavery had ended.

Meanwhile, in Europe other lands were coming together as nations. In central Europe there were many little states where people spoke German. Which famous storytellers encouraged Germans to realize they were really one people? [14]

The Grimms' fairy tales were works all Germans shared--no matter which state they lived in. But one man thought the Germans shouldn't be divided into many states. They should live together as a nation. He led Prussia. What was his name? [15]

In Italy another leader wanted to unite his native land. Remember that Italy, the boot-like peninsula pointing into the Mediterranean Sea, was made up of many city-states. But Italians could think back to the glory days of Rome, when they had all been united under one empire. Why not unite again? Which leader fought with his Red Shirts to unite Italy into a single nation? [16]

By 1890, the modern nations of Germany and Italy had been born.

With all this pride in new nations, all of this "nationalism," people began to think about proving who was best! Sometimes, as we'll see soon, that meant they started wars with each other. But other times they looked for ways to compete peacefully. Which ancient games were revived in the 1800s to allow nations to compete in athletics? [17]

A Frenchman, Coubertin, organized these new Olympics. But where were the first modern Olympic Games held? [18]

Growing nations. Growing industry. Growing competition among nations. They would all make industrial nations think about expanding even more. That's our next story!

Activity 2: Online Interactive Review (Online)

ASSESS

Unit Assessment: The Growth of Nations (Offline)

You will complete an online assessment of the main objectives covered so far in this unit. Follow the instructions online. Your assessment will be scored by the computer.

Name _____ Date _____

The Growth of Nations

Fill in the bubble in front of the best answer for each question.

1. I was a Russian czar who traveled through western Europe, then tried to bring western ways to my country. Who am I?

   Ⓐ   Peter the Great

   Ⓑ   Garibaldi

   Ⓒ   von Bismarck

   Ⓓ   Nicholas I

2. I was born a German noble, but ruled Russia in the eighteenth century. I liked western ideas. I expanded Russia to the Black Sea. Who am I?

   Ⓐ   Peter the Great

   Ⓑ   Otto von Bismarck

   Ⓒ   Karl Marx

   Ⓓ   Catherine the Great

3. I ruled harshly in Russia. I dedicated my reign to stop the spread of western ideas into Russia. I was called the policeman of Europe. Who am I?

   Ⓐ   Peter the Great

   Ⓑ   Nicholas I

   Ⓒ   Giuseppe Garibaldi

   Ⓓ   Baron de Coubertin

4. What was happening in Russia in the early 1800s?

   Ⓐ   Democratic revolutions were overthrowing the czars

   Ⓑ   Ideas about liberty and revolutions were spreading to Russia

   Ⓒ   The czars were keeping the Industrial Revolution from spreading to Russia

   Ⓓ   Russian military leaders were invading China and Japan

5. The modern Olympic games have their origins in _____.

   Ⓐ   eighteenth century America

   Ⓑ   medieval England

   Ⓒ   ancient Rome

   Ⓓ   ancient Greece

6. Which of the following best describes the Olympics?

   Ⓐ   A military competition between Greeks in which citizens compete in combat

   Ⓑ   An international athletic competition in which nations compete peacefully

   Ⓒ   An economic competition between factory owners and private citizens

   Ⓓ   An international competition in which nations fight one another in war games

7. I was president of the United States during the Civil War. I was committed to saving the Union. Who am I?

   Ⓐ   George Washington

   Ⓑ   Thomas Jefferson

   Ⓒ   Abraham Lincoln

   Ⓓ   Theodore Roosevelt

8. Which phrase describes the economy in the Southern states in the United States in 1860?

   (A)   Small farms and free laborers

   (B)   Large cities and great industry

   (C)   Plantation agriculture and slave labor

   (D)   Free laborers and trade with France

9. Which phrase describes economy in the Northern states in the United States. in 1860?

   (A)   Free labor, plantation agriculture, and cotton production

   (B)   Large farms and slave labor

   (C)   Slave labor and factories

   (D)   Growing industry, small farms, and free labor

10. What issue divided the North from the South in 1860?

   (A)   The role the United States should take in European affairs

   (B)   The expansion of slavery into new territories

   (C)   The use of factories to produce goods

   (D)   The rise of nationalism in the Eastern hemisphere

11. What happened soon after Abraham Lincoln was elected president?

   (A)   Slavery was abolished in all the Southern states.

   (B)   Northern states refused to accept Lincoln as president.

   (C)   Several Southern states seceded from the Union.

   (D)   The North sent troops to attack cities in the South.

12. The Civil War is the war that _____.

    Ⓐ   ended slavery and divided the United States into two separate nations

    Ⓑ   kept the United States from expanding westward, across the Mississippi River

    Ⓒ   made the United States a major world power

    Ⓓ   ended slavery and confirmed the United States as a single nation

13. What was the Gettysburg Address?

    Ⓐ   The place where Lincoln lived when not at the White House

    Ⓑ   An important speech Lincoln gave at the end of the Battle of Gettysburg

    Ⓒ   A major battle between the North and South during the Civil War

    Ⓓ   The location of the Union army's headquarters in Pennsylvania

14. When the Brothers Grimm were writing, Germany was _____.

    Ⓐ   united into a single nation under a strong monarch

    Ⓑ   a land in which most people spoke German

    Ⓒ   made up of many different kingdoms

    Ⓓ   both A and B

    Ⓔ   both B and C

15. Who wanted to promote a sense of national identity and pride among the German people?

Ⓐ   Peter the Great

Ⓑ   Giuseppe Garibaldi

Ⓒ   the Grimm brothers

Ⓓ   the Russian czars

16. Which was the most powerful German kingdom?

Ⓐ   Bavaria

Ⓑ   Westphalia

Ⓒ   Prussia

Ⓓ   Hanover

17. Otto von Bismarck was a(n) _____.

Ⓐ   Italian dictator who united Italy into a single nation

Ⓑ   Prussian statesman who united Germany into a single nation

Ⓒ   German monarch who resisted the unification of Germany

Ⓓ   German author who collected German folktales

18. I was a military leader who fought to _____ Italy. Who am I?

Ⓐ   unite; Giuseppe Garibaldi

Ⓑ   rule; Giuseppe Garibaldi

Ⓒ   divide up; Alexander Ypsilanti

Ⓓ   conquer; Peter the Great

19. These two European nations had been made up of many little states, but they became large single nations in the nineteenth century. Which nations were they?

    Ⓐ   Germany and France

    Ⓑ   Italy and England

    Ⓒ   England and Russia

    Ⓓ   Italy and Germany

20. Write a short paragraph about nationalism. In your paragraph:

    - Describe or define *nationalism*.
    - Identify two important people who promoted nationalism.
    - Give two consequences, or results, of the rise of nationalism. In other words, what happened because of the rise of nationalism?

Begin your paragraph with a topic sentence. Write neatly in complete sentences. Check your spelling, capitalization, and punctuation. End your paragraph with a concluding sentence.

_____

_____

_____

_____

_____

_____

_____

_____

Student Guide
Lesson 14: Semester Assessment

You've completed the first semester, so now it's time to take the semester assessment.

Lesson Objectives

- Demonstrate mastery of important knowledge and skills learned this semester.
- Demonstrate mastery of important knowledge and skills taught in previous lessons.
- Explain that Locke believed that if rulers governed badly, the people had a right of revolution.
- Identify Thomas Jefferson as the author of the Declaration of Independence.
- Identify the Constitutional Convention as the meeting in which the United States made a new plan of government.
- Describe Napoleon as the republican hero who became an all-powerful emperor.
- Explain that some colonists desired independence as they watched events in the young United States and in France.
- Explain that Bolívar led military campaigns to free much of Spanish America and is known as "the Liberator."
- Name capitalism as a system in which individuals and private companies make decisions about the economy.
- Explain that Marx predicted a revolution in which the working classes would rise up and overthrow the owners of industry.
- Recognize that the terms *Marxism* and *communism* refer to the work and theories of Karl Marx.
- Name Victoria as the British queen who reigned during this period.
- Describe Peter the Great as a czar who tried to bring western ways to Russia.
- Describe the Civil War as the war that ended slavery and confirmed that the United States was a single nation.
- Identify Abraham Lincoln as president of the United States during the Civil War.
- Recognize that the Brothers Grimm wanted to promote a sense of national identity and pride.
- Recall that Germany was made up of many kingdoms.
- Identify Otto von Bismarck as a Prussian statesman who united Germany into a single nation.
- Explain that Italy was once divided into many city-states and kingdoms.
- Name Great Britain's economy as the first capitalist economy.
- Recognize that Watt's steam engine could be used to power many machines.
- Name the American and French Revolutions as two great democratic revolutions.
- Describe a constitution as the basic law of government, which sets up the form of the government.
- Describe the Terror as a time of violence when many "enemies of the revolution" were killed.
- Explain that the French Revolution led to major European wars.
- Identify key figures, documents, and events in the American and French Revolutions (John Locke, Thomas Jefferson, James Madison, George Washington, Lafayette, Louis XVI, Robespierre, Napoleon, the Declaration of Independence, the U.S. Constitution, storming the Bastille, the Napoleonic Code, Waterloo).
- Explain that the Industrial Revolution began in England.

- Explain that during the Industrial Revolution production moved out of the home and into factories.
- Explain that in the early stages of the Industrial Revolution working conditions were harsh and workers suffered.
- Identify important figures, inventions, and ideas of the Industrial Revolution (James Watt, Robert Fulton, Charles Dickens, Karl Marx, spinning jenny, steam engine, steamboat, railroads, capitalism, Marxism).
- Describe the spread of democratic revolution to Latin America.
- Identify key figures and events of major revolutions in Latin America (including Toussaint L'Ouverture, Francisco Miranda, Miguel Hidalgo, Simon Bolívar).
- Describe the Scientific Revolution as a time of great progress in understanding nature.
- Explain that scientists used new methods of experimentation, obversation, and mathematics to understand nature.
- Identify key figures in the Scientific Revolution (Harvey, Hooke, Leeuwenhoek, Descartes, Newton, Franklin) and their contributions.
- Explain that people gained confidence in their ability to understand the laws of nature.

PREPARE

Approximate lesson time is 60 minutes.

LEARN

Activity 1: The Growth of Nations (Offline)

Instructions

We've covered a lot, and now it's time to take a look back. Here's what you should remember from the first semester.

Do you feel as if you've run a long race? You should. We've sped through three centuries. We've covered at least four revolutions--scientific, democratic, industrial, and national. Whew! Is your heart pumping wildly? Well, travel back in time and ask Dr. Harvey for an explanation.

You remember William Harvey, don't you? He was physician to King James. Dr. Harvey studied hearts--the hearts of frogs, deer, and humans, too. He experimented carefully. He looked at things closely. He figured out the heart is a pump that pushes blood to all parts of the human body.

At the beginning of our course, Dr. Harvey introduced us to a new way of studying nature--a new method of figuring things out. What is that method called? [1]

The scientific method is an organized way to study nature. It gave us modern science. The first scientists did experiments, observed closely, wrote things down, and reasoned about what they saw.

They looked for laws of nature. In the 1600s and 1700s, some scientists got so good at it that human understanding of nature shot forward. It was a big change. We call it the Scientific Revolution.

The Scientific Revolution brought us the microscope, Cartesian coordinates, and Newton's laws of planetary motion. It brought us Ben Franklin's work on electricity. It brought us Denis Diderot's "electrifying" attempt to write about all these advances in an encyclopedia.

Other revolutions were on the way. Some were democratic revolutions. In a way, the democratic revolutions sprang from the Scientific Revolution. After all, if human beings could figure out basic laws of nature, couldn't they also figure out basic laws of government? Wasn't it true that human beings had basic rights that rulers should respect?

Maybe the people should protect their own rights by ruling themselves!

Those were bold ideas in the 1700s. Self rule! Democracy! Americans liked them. "We hold these truths to be self-evident, that all men are created equal, that they are endowed by their Creator with certain unalienable rights, that among these are life, liberty, and the pursuit of happiness." With those words Americans announced their revolution to the world. Who wrote them? [2] Where do you find those words? [3]

The ideas that "all men are created equal" and that human beings had rights no one could take from them were sheer dynamite. Those ideas exploded all over the world.

Which great democratic revolution erupted in Europe after the American Revolution? [4]

The French stormed the Bastille in Paris and got rid of their king. But they weren't lucky with their constitutions. The French didn't worry about checks and balances, like the Americans did. A bloody period known as the Terror and then a dictatorship followed. Which Frenchman, who became emperor and dictator in the early 1800s, soon took Europe by storm? [5]

Napoléon set up a new code of laws for France. He tried to spread the revolution to the rest of Europe. Fifteen years later he met his Waterloo! What does that mean? [6]

You can defeat a general. You can defeat a nation. But it's hard to defeat good ideas. Those ideas of self-government and rule of the people swept to Latin America.

By the 1820s, most of Latin America was free from French and Spanish rule. Sadly, military dictators seemed to replace kings there as they had in France. Was revolution over?

Not quite. Something was happening in the towns and villages of Great Britain. Looms were whirring. Boats were chugging. Smoke was belching along railroad tracks. This was a different kind of revolution--an Industrial Revolution.

Machines drove this revolution. Great Britain began to fill up with spinning jennies, steam engines, steam boats, railroads, power looms, and for the first time, factories.

Ordinary workers stopped making things in their homes and started working in factories. In factories big machines could be grouped together.

Those first factories were dark, unpleasant places. Machines clattered. Children worked alongside adults. Everyone worked to a clock. Most people worked 10- or 12-hour days.

The factories were not very nice places to work. But they did make it possible to make more things faster. Machines could make all sorts of goods in factories.

Some people made a lot of money from the new factories and goods. A middle class sprang up. And those who owned the factories became rich. As Charles Dickens might have said, for some it was the best of times, for others the worst of times.

England sped ahead of the rest of Europe with her industry and inventions. Her new system of capitalism made her very productive.

A German thinker in London watched it all happen. He said capitalism would eventually destroy itself because the owners got too much and the workers too little.

He said that soon there would be a revolution by workers. Who was that German thinker? [7]

Marx said that someday the factories would belong to everyone, not just a few rich people. He predicted that property and wealth would be held in common by all the people. What did he call this idea? [8]

While the German, Karl Marx, was in England writing about communism, his homeland was being united.

We've just learned that the 1800s were a time when little states in Europe came together as nations. Bismark helped unite Germany. Garibaldi helped turn Italy into one nation. In the United States, meanwhile, Abraham Lincoln led the nation through a war to save the Union.

By the end of the 1800s, some big ideas and some big revolutions had taken hold.

People were learning more about nature. They were using that knowledge about nature to increase industry. People were learning more about their rights and how to protect rights with democratic governments. Serfdom had ended. Slavery had ended. New nations had been born. At the Olympic Games, nations competed and began to know each other--they would learn a lot more about each other in the years to come.

Activity 2: End of Semester *(Online)*

ASSESS

Semester Assessment: History 4, Semester 1 (*Offline*)

Complete an offline Semester Assessment. Your learning coach will score this part of the assessment.

Name_____   Date_____

Semester Assessment

Read each question and the possible answers. Fill in the bubble in front of the best answer.

1. How would you describe the Scientific Revolution of the 1600s and 1700s?

   ⓐ A period when many nations overthrew kings

   ⓑ An age when computers became important

   ⓒ A time of great progress in understanding nature

   ⓓ A time when industry moved from factory to the home

2. The scientific method requires _____.

   ⓐ expensive equipment and modern computers

   ⓑ careful observation, experimentation, mathematics, and reason

   ⓒ dedication to the fields of biology and astronomy

   ⓓ spells and incantations, omens and charms, many trials and errors

3. Two important thinkers during the Scientific Revolution were

   ⓐ Newton and Descartes

   ⓑ L'Ouverture and Hidalgo

   ⓒ Marx and Dickens

   ⓓ Watt and Fulton

4. The discoveries of the Scientific Revolution gave people

    (a)   new hope that kings and queens would fund research.

    (b)   worries about the difficult future before them.

    (c)   more evidence that the Sun rotated around Earth.

    (d)   new confidence in their ability to understand the laws of nature.

5. John Locke tried to understand the laws of government. What did he teach?

    (a)   Only nobles and royalty have rights.

    (b)   Monarchs have the power to get rid of Parliament.

    (c)   If rulers govern badly, people have a right to revolt.

    (d)   Workers should rebel against factory owners.

6. Two great democratic revolutions erupted in the late 1700s. Where did they occur?

    (a)   England and the United States

    (b)   The United States and France

    (c)   Spain and France

    (d)   Greece and Germany

7. What is a constitution?

    (a)   The basic budget of a nation, establishing the limits of spending and debt

    (b)   A document that shows the borders of each state in the nation

    (c)   The statements that declare a colony's independence from its mother country

    (d)   The basic law of government, establishing the form of a country's government

8. In a document called the _____ , written by
_____ , the United States of America announced
its independence to the world.

   ⓐ   U.S. Constitution; James Madison

   ⓑ   Magna Carta; King John

   ⓒ   Declaration of Independence; Thomas Jefferson

   ⓓ   Mayflower Compact; William Bradford

9. What happened at the Constitutional Convention in 1787?

   ⓐ   The Third Estate in France formed a new government.

   ⓑ   The United States made a new plan of government.

   ⓒ   The United States declared independence from Great Britain.

   ⓓ   A large crowd stormed the Bastille and demanded
          a constitution.

10. What was the Terror and who rose to power after it ended?

   ⓐ   A time when monarchs were overthrown; Thomas Jefferson

   ⓑ   A time of terrible violence in France; Napoleon Bonaparte

   ⓒ   The battle in which Napoleon was defeated; Robespierre

   ⓓ   A warning to keep out of Europe's affairs; George Washington

11. How did the French Revolution affect the rest of Europe?

   ⓐ   It had almost no effect because the French people and armies
          kept to themselves.

   ⓑ   Many nations admired Napoleon and eagerly made
          him emperor.

   ⓒ   The French tried to spread their revolution and a period of
          wars followed.

   ⓓ   Some nations provided a new home for Louis XVI.

12. Soon after the American and French Revolutions, ideas of self-government and rule of the people spread to which region of the world?

   (a) Africa

   (b) Asia

   (c) Latin America

   (d) Middle East

13. By the 1820s, most of _____ had won its independence from _____ .

   (a) Africa; France

   (b) Asia; England

   (c) Latin America; Spain

   (d) Middle East; Germany

14. Who was known as the "Liberator" of South America?

   (a) Miguel Hidalgo

   (b) Bernardo O'Higgins

   (c) Simón Bolivar

   (d) José de San Martín

15. Great Britain was the birthplace of a "revolution" driven by powerful machines. More and more people stopped making things in their homes and started working in factories. What was this change called?

   (a) The computer age

   (b) The machine age

   (c) The Scientific Revolution

   (d) The Industrial Revolution

16. Which invention made it possible to power boats and locomotives as well as looms?

- (a) Macadam
- (b) Spinning jenny
- (c) Steam engine
- (d) Railroads

17. During the early Industrial Revolution, what were working conditions like for factory workers?

- (a) The hours were long and the factories were dark and unsafe.
- (b) The factories were well lit and clean, but the hours were long.
- (c) Women and children worked few hours, but men worked long hours.
- (d) The pay was good, and most people were quite happy.

18. In what economic system are individuals and private companies in charge of making economic choices?

- (a) Communism
- (b) Socialism
- (c) Traditionalism
- (d) Capitalism

19. Which philosopher believed capitalism would eventually destroy itself? He wrote about class struggle and the revolt of workers against business owners.

- (a) James Hargreaves
- (b) Karl Marx
- (c) Charles Dickens
- (d) Prince Albert

20. Which very productive country had the world's first capitalist economy?

    ⓐ   France

    ⓑ   Portugal

    ⓒ   Germany

    ⓓ   Great Britain

21. Karl Marx's idea that property and wealth should be held in common by all the people is called _____.

    ⓐ   communism

    ⓑ   traditionalism

    ⓒ   capitalism

    ⓓ   federalism

22. Who ruled England at the height of the Industrial Revolution?

    ⓐ   Prince Albert

    ⓑ   King George III

    ⓒ   Queen Victoria

    ⓓ   Catherine the Great

23. He was so excited about the Scientific and Industrial Revolutions in the west that he tried to bring western ways to Russia. Who was he?

    ⓐ   Peter the Great

    ⓑ   Nicholas II

    ⓒ   Prince Albert

    ⓓ   Karl Marx

24. Bismarck united many small states into this single nation. And the Brothers Grimm collected fairy tales to help give the people a sense of national identity. What place was this?

  (a) Germany

  (b) France

  (c) Italy

  (d) Russia

25. Which two European nations had been many little states until they became large single nations in the nineteenth century?

  (a) Italy and England

  (b) England and Russia

  (c) Italy and Germany

  (d) Germany and France

26. Who was the U.S. president during the Civil War?

  (a) George Washington

  (b) Thomas Jefferson

  (c) Abraham Lincoln

  (d) Theodore Roosevelt

27. The Civil War is the war that _____.

  (a) ended slavery and confirmed the United States as a single nation

  (b) ended slavery and divided the United States into two separate nations

  (c) kept the United States from expanding westward, across the Mississippi River

  (d) made the United States a major world power

Match each revolution on the left with the people on the right who played important roles in the revolution.

28. _____ Scientific   A. James Watt, Robert Fulton

    _____ Democratic   B. William Harvey, Isaac Newton

    _____ Industrial   C. Thomas Jefferson, Simon Bolivar